THE CIVILISATION OF SWEDEN

IN

HEATHEN TIMES

THE
CIVILISATION OF SWEDEN
IN HEATHEN TIMES

BY

OSCAR MONTELIUS, Ph.D.

PROFESSOR AT THE NATIONAL HISTORICAL MUSEUM, STOCKHOLM

TRANSLATED FROM THE SECOND SWEDISH EDITION
REVISED AND ENLARGED BY THE AUTHOR

BY

REV. F. H. WOODS, B.D.

Vicar of Chalfont St. Peter

WITH MAP AND TWO HUNDRED AND FIVE ILLUSTRATIONS

HASKELL HOUSE PUBLISHERS Ltd.
Publishers of Scarce Scholarly Books
NEW YORK, N. Y. 10012
1969

First Published 1888

HASKELL HOUSE PUBLISHERS Ltd.
Publishers of Scarce Scholarly Books
280 LAFAYETTE STREET
NEW YORK, N. Y. 10012

Library of Congress Catalog Card Number: 68-25251

Standard Book Number 8383-0216-5

Printed in the United States of America

TRANSLATOR'S PREFACE.

THE name of Dr. Montelius is too well known in archæological circles to make any apology for translating such a work as this necessary.

The book describes the early progress of Swedish civilisation from a time some thousands of years anterior to history, if by that term is meant only what depends upon written documents. But, as the writer shows, the evidence of history in this limited sense is often far less trustworthy than that on which the antiquary relies. The latter has at least the advantage of being in all cases contemporary, and therefore less liable to perversion. But its chief value is that it helps to throw light upon periods of man's development on which history is altogether silent, and of which we have therefore no sources of information. It is true that it deals directly with the progress of one particular people; but all archæology tends to show that there has been a remarkably similar process of development, not only among European peoples, but among all races of the world. It follows that a clear and succinct account of the progress of any one people helps to give us a clear notion of the successive stages of civilisation through which all races have passed. For Englishmen the work is likely to have a special interest, partly from the close relationship between the Swedish and English nationalities, but still more because of the direct influence of the Scandinavian races upon the history of England from the time when the Northmen first harried our coasts.

The second edition of this work was published in Swedish in 1878, but afterwards appeared in 1885 in a much enlarged German translation, with many additional plates. The present edition contains all the additional matter incorporated in the German translation; but besides this the author has again made many important additions and introduced several new plates. It thus embodies the results of researches made since 1885 down to the current year (1888). The proof-sheets have been revised throughout by the author, whose kindness and enthusiasm have lightened the work of translation, and deepened the interest which work in a subject of this kind can hardly fail to excite. The translator has, with the author's consent, ventured to add a few references or explanations which he felt likely to be of interest to an English reader. These are inclosed in square brackets, usually in the form of footnotes. He has made frequent reference especially to the *Corpus Poeticum Boreale* of Dr. Vigfusson and Mr.

Powell, whose work he has found of great value in enabling him to give a more accurate rendering of quotations from Icelandic poems. He begs also to take this opportunity of acknowledging his indebtedness to Dr. Evans, whose great work on the Bronze Age [1] has supplied him with many technical terms. While avoiding what seemed an unnecessary use of technical language, he has in general adopted expressions most frequently used by English archæologists. In the translation of *gånggrifter* by "passage-graves" he has purposely departed from this rule, because the usual English term, "gallery-graves," to say nothing of its uncouth sound, seemed to express a wrong idea. The word "gallery" suggests to his mind something of the nature of a gallery in a theatre or a church, and to be little suited to express the simple underground passage which formed part of the graves of this description.

[1] *The Ancient Bronze Implements, Weapons, and Ornaments of Great Britain and Ireland:* London, 1881.

CHALFONT ST. PETER VICARAGE,
October 4th, 1888.

CONTENTS.

	PAGE
INTRODUCTION	1

CHAPTER I.
THE STONE AGE 7

CHAPTER II.
THE BRONZE AGE 42

CHAPTER III.
THE IRON AGE 89
    A. THE FIRST PART OF THE EARLIER IRON AGE 91
    B. THE SECOND PART OF THE EARLIER IRON AGE 97
    C. THE FIRST PART OF THE LATER IRON AGE 125
    D. THE SECOND PART OF THE LATER IRON AGE, OR THE VIKING PERIOD 142

LIST OF ILLUSTRATIONS.

FIG.		PAGE
1.	Flint tool of the earlier Stone Age	9
2.	,, ,, ,,	9
3.	Hammering-pebble	12
4.	Section of a haft-hole in stone axe	13
5.	Section of a half-finished haft-hole	13
6.	Axe-head of greenstone, with hole partly bored	14
7.	Flint arrow-head	14
8.	Small gouge, polished	14
9.	Unpolished flint-axe	14
10.	Polished grindstone	14
11.	Flint spear-head	15
12.	Flint-scraper	15
13.	Flint knife	15
14.	Stone axe with haft-hole	15
15.	Lunate flint saw	15
16.	Flint dagger	17
17.	Plan of a Lap dwelling (*gamme*) at Komagfjord in North Finmark, near Hammerfest	19
18.	Stone axe with wooden handle found in an English bog	20
19.	Flint axe showing marks where the haft was fastened	21
20.	Stone axe with wooden handle from New Caledonia	21
21.	Flint scraper	21
22.	Stone axe with haft-hole	24
23.	,, ,,	24
24.	Amber bead	25
25.	Bone arrow-head with flakes of flint let in on the sides	25
26.	Bone fish-hook	25
27.	Stone handmill	27
28.	South African handmill in use	28
29.	Clay hanging-cauldron	29
30.	Animal figure on a horn axe	29

LIST OF ILLUSTRATIONS.

FIG.		PAGE
31.	Dolmen at Haga, on the island of Orust	30
32.	Two passage-graves at Luttra	31
33.	Plan of a passage-grave near Falköping	32
34.	Stone cist near Skottened	33
35.	Stone cist near Karleby	34
36.	Plan of the stone cist described in Fig. 35	35
37.	Offering-stone	36
38.	Spear-head of slate	38
39.	Knife of slate	38
40.	Massive bronze axe with haft-hole	44
41.	Bronze dagger with handle of the same material	44
42.	Handle of dagger (Fig. 41) as seen from the top	44
43.	Lower part of the ferrule of a bronze spear-head	44
44.	*Fibula* of bronze	44
45.	Bronze knife	45
46.	End of a large bronze collar	45
47.	Upper part of the blade of a bronze sword	45
48.	Part of the bottom of a golden bowl	45
49.	Stone mould for casting four bronze saws like that in Fig. 50	49
50.	Bronze saw	49
51.	Bronze runner with four jets	50
52.	Bronze axe, of thin plates over clay core	52
53.	A celt (not socketed) fastened to the haft from a rock-carving of the Bronze Age	54
54.	Bronze socketed celt with wooden haft, found in a salt-mine at Hallein in Austria	55
55.	Egyptian bronze celt with wooden handle	55
56.	Bronze celt (not socketed)	56
57.	„ „	56
58.	Bronze celt (socketed)	56
59.	Gold tweezers	56
60.	Bronze button	56
61.	Spiral finger-ring of a double gold wire	56
62.	Gold bracelet	57
63.	Bronze torque	57
64.	Spiral bronze bracelet	57
65.	Bronze ornament with inlaid resin on the knob	58
66.	Piece of woollen stuff of the Bronze Age	59
67.	Tree-coffin of the Bronze Age, showing the body of a man wrapped in a woollen mantle, with the head towards the left	59
68.	Woman's woollen dress, from Borum-Eshöi	61
69.	Bronze *fibula*	64
70.	Bronze brooch	64

LIST OF ILLUSTRATIONS. xiii

FIG.
71. Bronze comb, with all the teeth broken off 65
72. Bronze torque 65
73. Bronze shield with *répoussé* ornaments, of foreign workmanship 66
74. Bronze sword 68
75. Bronze dagger with horn handle 68
76. Leather sheath with bronze chape for dagger 68
77. Bronze spear-head 68
78. Bronze sword with handle of the same material, of foreign workmanship 68
79. Plough from a rock-carving at Tegneby 71
80. Bronze sickle 71
81. }
82. } Parts of a bronze set of harness 72
83. }
84. }
85. } Boats from rock-carvings in Bohuslän 73
86. }
87. Rock-carving near Backa 74
88. Rock-carving in Lökeberg in Bohuslän 75
89. One of the stones of the grave at Kivik 76
90. Sword on a rock-carving at Ekensberg 77
91. Diminutive car which probably once carried a sacrificial vessel as here traced 79
92. Gold vessel 81
93. Large bronze vase found at Hedeskoga 82
94. Cover to bronze-vessel 83
95. Bronze hanging-vessel 83
96. Section of a barrow at Dömmestorp in South Halland . . . 85
97. Burial-urn with handle 86
98. Bronze brooch with an iron pin 92
99. Bronze collar 92
100. Bronze collar with a joint 92
101. Iron sword in a sheath of the same metal 93
102. Iron knife 93
103. Iron *fibula* 93
104. Bronze *fibula* 93
105. Bronze collar, with a joint 94
106. Iron plate for belt (?) overlaid with bronze 95
107. Bronze collar 95
108. Roman silver coin (denarius) 98
109. Bronze vessel dedicated to Apollo Grannus, of Roman workmanship 100
110. Part of an iron coat of mail 101

LIST OF ILLUSTRATIONS.

FIG.		PAGE
111.	Roman bronze statuette	102
112.	Glass beaker, of Roman workmanship	103
113.	Iron sword with maker's mark	104
114.	Spiral gold bracelet	105
115.	A horn with bronze mountings	107
116.	Northern warrior of about 300 A.D.	109
117.	*Fibula* of silver-gilt	110
118.	Bronze buckle, overlaid with silver-gilt and set with coloured glass	110
119.	Gold ring	111
120.	Gold pendant	111
121.	Silver cup partly gilded	112
122.	Wooden bucket with bronze platings	113
123.	Earthenware ewer	114
124.	Boat for 14 pairs of oars, found at Nydam in South Jutland	116
125.	Runic stone at Tanum in Bohuslän	120
126.	Cemetery near Greby in Bohuslän	123
127.	Roman gold coin (solidus)	125
128.	Gold collar	126
129.	Gold plate of a sword-sheath	127
130.	Gold collar with joint	128
131.	Gold bracteate with a list of runes	130
132.	Gold bracteate	130
133.	Gold finger-ring with one end broken off	130
134.	Gold bracteate, a "barbarian" copy of a Roman coin	130
135.	*Fibula* of silver-gilt	132
136.	Buckle of silver-gilt	133
137.	Reverse side of Fig. 136	134
138.	Upper part of an iron sword with hilt of gilded bronze. The triangular pommel is of gold inlaid with garnets	135
139.	Ornament of gilded bronze	136
140.	A plate of gilded bronze	136
141.	Upper part of an iron sword with hilt of gilded bronze	137
142.	Boss of a shield made of iron with bronze plating	138
143.	Chape of gilded bronze	139
144.	Part of a helmet made of iron overlaid with bronze	140
145.	Small oval *fibula* of gilded bronze	141
146.	Bronze key	152
147.	Glass cup	154
148.	Silver pendant	155
149.	Spoon made of elk-horn	156
150.	Piece of a woollen mantle with embroidery	158
151.	„ „ „ „	159

LIST OF ILLUSTRATIONS.

FIG.		PAGE
152.	A loom from the Färö Isles	160
153.	Bronze plate with figures in relief	162
154.	Oval bronze brooch	163
155.	Round bronze brooch	164
156.	Round silver brooch	164
157.	Silver brooch	165
158.	Bronze brooch of silver-gilt	166
159.	Bronze *fibula* (two views)	167
160.	Ring-shaped bronze brooch	167
161.	Solid silver bracelet	168
162.	Twisted silver bracelet	169
163–167.	Silver beads	169
168.	Silver pendant	169
169.	,, ,,	169
170.	Iron hammer	170
171.	Iron pincers	170
172.	Iron sickle	174
173.	Iron axe	180
174.	Upper part of a two-edged iron sword	181
175.	Part of a damasked sword-blade	182
176.	Grave-stone with carvings and runic inscription, from Tjängvide	183
177.	A Northman's ship from the end of the eleventh century, taken from the Bayeux tapestry	184
178.	An oak ship found in the barrow at Tune in South Norway	185
179.	Viking-ship *as found* at Gokstad, in South Norway	186
180.	The Gokstad ship *restored*	187
181.	Anglo-Saxon silver coin of King Æthelræd	189
182.	Earliest Swedish silver coin struck for Olaf Skötkonung	189
183.	Marble lion with runic inscription, originally in the Piræus, now at Venice. Height 9 ft.	190
184.	Arabic silver coin (*dirhem*) struck at Samarcand in A.D. 903	191
185.	German silver coin	192
186.	Pair of scales made of bronze	193
187.	Iron weight plated with bronze	193
188.	Iron stirrup	194
189.	Bronze buckle	195
190.	Bronze plate	196
191.	Gilded bronze plate that probably originally surrounded the foot of a drinking vessel	196

LIST OF ILLUSTRATIONS.

FIG.		PAGE
192.	Bronze brooch	197
193.	Bronze brooch, of the form of an animal's head	197
194.	Back of Fig. 193, with a runic inscription	197
195.	Two bronze buckles united with chains	198
196.	Gold bracteate	199
197.	The "Ramsundsberg" with the "Sigurd-carving"	201
198.	Silver "Thor's hammer"	202
199.	Barrow from the Viking Period	204
200.	Grave-stones arranged in the form of a ship; near Blomsholm in Bohuslän	206
201.	Plan of stones as arranged in Fig. 200	207
202.	Barrow with "bauta-stone" near Gödestad in Halland	208
203.	Runic-stone near Rök church in Öster-Götland	211
204.	Runic-stone at Viggby in Upland, 7 ft. high	212
205.	Runic-stone near Vik in Upland	213

ANCIENT SWEDISH CIVILISATION.

INTRODUCTION.

THE history of the earliest inhabitants of the North was till about fifty years ago shrouded in obscurity. It was not till then that antiquarians began generally to recognize that the antiquities which are dug up from time to time, and the barrows and stone monuments which still abound throughout the country, do not all belong to that part of heathen times which immediately preceded the introduction of Christianity, and of which the Icelandic sagas relate. When Ansgar first came to Sweden in the ninth century, the use of iron was universal in the country, and had been so for a long time. A careful investigation of the antiquities has shown however that before that period, now usually known as the Iron Age, there was another, when iron was altogether unknown, in which weapons and tools were made of bronze, a mixture of copper and tin. This period, called the Bronze Age, had, as well as the Iron Age, continued for many centuries. But before the beginning of the Bronze Age Sweden had for a very long time been inhabited by people who lived in entire ignorance of the use of the metals, and were therefore compelled to make their instruments and weapons of such materials as stone, horn, bone, and wood. This last period is known therefore as the Stone Age.

This division of heathen times in the North into three great periods was already made and published as long ago as the last century, but it was not till 1830-40 that it had any special importance in antiquarian researches. The honour of developing a scientific system based upon this triple division—a work so important for gaining an insight into the earliest condition of the whole human race—belongs to the *savants* of the North. The first place among them is occupied by Councillor Christian Jürgensen Thomsen (died 1865), to whose labours we are mainly indebted for the celebrated Museum of Northern Antiquities in Copenhagen. Next to him we must place as the founders of the prehistoric archæology of the north Professor Sven Nilsson of Lund (died 1883),[1] and Chamberlain J. J. À. Worsaae (died 1885). Thomsen's system was soon taken up by the Royal Antiquary Bror Emil Hildebrand (died 1884), who did the greatest service by his development of the National Historical Museum at Stockholm. The "three-age-system" was also quickly adopted in almost every other country. The attack long made against it in Germany may now be regarded as ceased, and the correctness of this division has been generally recognized even in that country.

[1] The first edition of his epoch-making work *Skandinaviska Nordens Urinvånare* appeared in 1838-43, the second in 1862-6. An English translation of this work, with a preface by Sir John Lubbock, was published in 1868 under the title *The Primitive Inhabitants of Scandinavia*.

The thousands of finds which have come to our knowledge since this system was published, have not only proved in a striking manner that the outline of the earliest history of Northern culture which antiquarians endeavoured to draw more than fifty years ago was correct, but have also opened a new and wide field for further research. We can now form a very clear idea of the circumstances under which the first settlers in our land lived, and we can follow, step by step, the slow but sure development whereby the inhabitants of Sweden, once a horde of savages, have reached their present condition.

It is true that we meet with no line of kings, no heroic names dating from these earliest times. But is not the knowledge of the people's life, and of the progress of their culture, of more worth than the names of saga heroes? And ought we not to give more credence to the contemporary, irrefutable witnesses to which alone archæology now listens, than to the poetical stories which for centuries were preserved only in the memory of skalds?

It might seem unnecessary at present to give any special proof of the correctness of this threefold division of heathen times in the North, inasmuch as the whole account we shall give may be regarded as proving it. But as the present position of Northern archæology depends so peculiarly upon this division, we shall now point out some circumstances which show how well grounded the opinion is, at least so far as Scandinavia is concerned.

That there was a time when all metals were entirely unknown is clearly seen from the many large finds and the hundreds of remarkable graves containing numerous relics of stone, bone, &c., but no trace of metal. That there was another period when the use of bronze, but not of iron, was known, is equally clear from the large number of hoards and graves which contain weapons, ornaments, &c., of bronze, but no trace of iron; while on the other hand bronze implements are hardly ever found with those of iron. That there was a third period in heathen times when iron was in general use we can see by the first glance at any large collection of antiquities. From this it follows of necessity that the earliest history of Northern culture—the time antecedent to the establishment of Christianity—actually embraces the three great periods which derive their names from the most important material in use during each of them.

And there can hardly be any doubt of the order in which these periods followed each other. That the Stone Age must be older than the Bronze Age is self-evident, and is further proved by the fact that we often find graves of the Bronze Age in the upper part of barrows which have been raised over a grave chamber of the Stone Age which usually lies at the bottom in the centre of the barrow, while the converse has never occurred. And our earliest sources of history which throw light on the conditions of life during the last part of heathen times point only to a period when iron was in general use. It follows therefore that the Iron Age must be the last of these three periods.

How far the beginning of each period coincides with the appearance of a new race which subdued the earlier settlers in the country, is a further question which we must for the present distinguish from that which concerns only the order in which the several heathen periods followed each other.

Before we now make an attempt to set before

our readers a picture of the life in Sweden during heathen times, we must observe that if that picture shall prove imperfect and blurred, it is partly perhaps owing to the insufficiency of our sources of information about a period so wanting in written historical materials. It is doubtless true, and should be gladly acknowledged, that we have discovered much richer documents dating from heathen times than we had any right to expect; but by far the majority of the antiquities preserved to our own day are naturally works of stone, metals, and the like, while it is only by an exceptional conjunction of specially favourable conditions that such perishable materials as wood, bone, leather, cloth, &c., have been able to survive. It follows that we must have a very imperfect knowledge of furniture, stuffs, and clothes made out of such materials; and yet these formed incomparably the greater part of the belongings of the heathen Northmen. But even of metal and stone objects used in those days our knowledge is very imperfect. Only a small part of what once existed was buried in the ground; only a part of what was buried has escaped the destroying hand of time; of this part all has not yet come to light again; and we know only too well how little of what has come to light has been of any service for our science. Almost all the finds of past centuries have disappeared without a trace, and even much of what has been discovered in the present century has been destroyed.

We can easily realize the importance of these facts if we imagine that an antiquarian some thousand or two thousand years hence should attempt to represent our own manner of life, and yet had scarcely any other material for the purpose beyond the verdigrised and rusty remains of our metal works, and so could not complete the picture of the nineteenth century by the help of works of literature and art. This comparison shows how cautious we should be in our attempt to trace the civilisation of heathen times, the earliest part of which was several thousand years before our day.

CHAPTER I.

THE STONE AGE.

(*To about* B.C. 1500.)

How long ago Sweden was inhabited we cannot yet decide, even within a thousand years. A number of finds have shown, it is true, that the south part of Scandinavia was peopled far earlier than was formerly supposed. But all we can do is to fix a point of time *before* which we can hardly suppose any settlement to have been made, namely, the end of the Glacial Period. So long as the Scandinavian peninsula was covered by one enormous mass of ice, just as the greater part of Greenland is at the present day, population was almost impossible, and no traces of men have been found in the country which are earlier than the end of this period.

On the other hand several finds have shown that Denmark and the most southerly part of Sweden were already inhabited by a people of the Stone Age at a time when firs were still the prevailing trees in those countries. For instance, bones of the capercailzie, a bird which only lives in fir woods, have been discovered in finds belonging indisputably to the Stone Age in Denmark. We cannot it is true determine, within a hundred or even a thousand years, how old these finds are; but that they must belong to a very remote period is shown by the thorough change in the flora and fauna which the country has since undergone. The forests of fir-trees died out, and made way for great forests of oaks, which covered the land, till they in their turn succumbed to the now prevailing beech woods.

The earliest traces of human remains yet known in Sweden are some large and very rough flint tools (Guide, Fig. 28), similar to what are met with in England and other countries in finds of the earliest Stone Age.

Traces of population in the North at a somewhat later, but still very early, date are found in the numerous Danish "kitchen-middens" (*kjökkenmöddinger*) or "refuse heaps" (*afskrädeshögar*), which for some time past have been the object of thorough investigation. These are found along the sea-coasts, and consist of, sometimes enormous, collections of the shells of oysters and other shell-fish still used for food at the present day. We also find in them bones of fish, birds, wild boar, red and fallow deer, ure-ox, and other wild animals,[1] but of only one domestic animal—the dog. The larger bones are usually found split open for the sake of the marrow. Among these relics of food materials we find also the fireplaces still charred and covered with ashes, and further a number of ill-hewn, unpolished flint tools, bits of coarse earthenware, instruments of bone and horn, &c. In the places where these "kitchen-middens" are found it is clear that men must have lived in far distant

[1] No traces of reindeer, which during a part of the Stone Age lived together with men in Belgium and France, have been met with in the Danish "kitchen-middens."

times: the shells, the bones, and the fireplaces are relics of their meals.

"Kitchen-middens" of precisely the same kind have been found in many other parts of the world, as, for example, in Terra del Fuego in the extreme south of

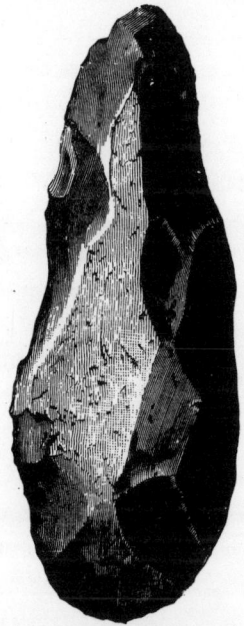

Fig. 1.—Flint tool of the earlier Stone Age. Sk. ½.

Fig. 2.—Flint tool of the earlier Stone Age. Sk. ½.

America, where the rude natives still live in much the same way as the earliest inhabitants of the North did several thousand years ago.

No "kitchen-middens" belonging to the Stone Age[1] have been hitherto discovered in Sweden; but we may

[1] Both in Sweden and in other countries traces of meals—refuse-heaps—have been found very much like the Danish "kitchen-middens," but they are later than the Stone Age.

be quite sure that the most southern part of this country was inhabited at the time to which these belong, because several rough flint tools have been found there, in Skåne especially, exactly resembling those usual in the "kitchen-middens" (see Figs. 1 and 2).

The Danish "kitchen-middens," and the finds corresponding to them, must be regarded as belonging to an earlier part of the Stone Age than those graves known as "dolmens" (*stendösar*) and "passage-graves" (*gånggrifter*), of which we shall soon speak. Of this we may give the following proofs—

1. In the "kitchen-middens" we find no traces of any other domestic animal than the dog, while the people of the passage-graves had all the most important domestic animals of the present day.

2. The flint instruments found in the "kitchen-middens" are generally much coarser than those which occur in the graves. They are of altogether different and much simpler forms, and *not polished;* the axes and chisels, well polished on all sides, which are so numerous in the graves, have never been met with in the "kitchen-middens." Neither do we find in the latter any of the well-hewn spear-heads or arrow-heads of flint (comp. Figs. 7, 11). Such things as chips and the like, incidental to the making of stone tools, and the simple flint flakes used for knives, and the rude flint scrapers are, as we might have expected, common to finds of every period within the Stone Age.

If remains of the earlier Stone Age are scanty in Sweden, we have on the contrary very abundant relics of its later part. With the exception of Denmark, and possibly that part of North Germany of which the antiquities belonging to the Stone and Bronze Ages are almost exactly like those of Scandinavia, there is probably no European land which can show such rich and beautiful relics from the later Stone Age as the southern part of Sweden.

Before we attempt to give any description of what is now known of primitive Swedish civilisation during the Stone Age, it would be as well first to show how it was possible out of the hard flint—the most important material of the time for weapons and tools—to prepare such wonderfully fine works without the help of metal.

Professor Nilsson, about fifty years ago, pointed out that flint could be easily worked with stone, and made drawings of some pebbles which he supposed to have been used for such a purpose. They had caught his attention because, as a boy when out shooting, he had often prepared his gun-flints with a stone picked up from the field.

Confirmations of Professor Nilsson's opinion have not been wanting. Some time ago an Englishman came across an Indian tribe in California, which still used stone implements. The Englishman was acquainted with the objects from the Stone Age found in Europe, but thought that they were prepared with tools of hardened copper. He now met with one of the arrow-head makers belonging to the tribe, and requested to be allowed to see some proof of his skill. The Indian sat down, laid a smooth stone on his knee, took in one hand a piece of agate, in the other a piece of obsidian, a species of stone which is used by the natives of America much as flint was by those of Europe. With one stroke of the agate he split the piece of obsidian in two, and with a second against the new surface thus made, he struck off a flake a third of an inch thick. This he took between his finger and thumb, held it against the stone anvil which lay on his knee, and gave it repeated blows with the agate, each blow taking off a minute chip. By degrees the piece of obsidian received a definite shape, and in a little more than an hour's time he had completed an arrow-head which was more than an inch long.

We know that not very long ago flint was used in preparing gun-locks and strike-a-lights in England and France. Iron hammers were then employed, but experience clearly shows that a common sea-worn pebble may be used with success. Besides, both in the North and in other lands, stones have been found which were obviously used in the Stone Age as chipping-stones in the preparation of flint. Sometimes they made small, round cup-shaped holes in the stone in order to secure a firmer grip for the fingers (see Fig. 3).

FIG. 3.—Hammering-pebble. Boh. ½.

The long and narrow barbs in the fine arrowheads (Fig. 7), and such regular serratures as we find for example in Fig. 15, were obtained probably by the stroke or pressure of a bone tool like those used for the same purpose by several American tribes.

Knives, daggers, spear-heads and arrow-heads, scrapers and other flint instruments of this kind, were only chipped and never ground, at least not at the edge. Many other stone implements however, especially axes and chisels, were ground, and we have still remaining a large number of grindstones used for this purpose. They are most usually either very large blocks of sandstone with one or more flat sides, or else thick pieces of a similar material shaped much like a club and rounded off at the two ends (see Fig. 10). Upon the former the flint axes (Fig. 9) and the broader chisels were ground; upon the latter narrow chisels, like that given in Fig. 8, and other small tools. By constant use on all its sides a grindstone of this sort became very narrow in the middle, and it is not surprising that it has some-

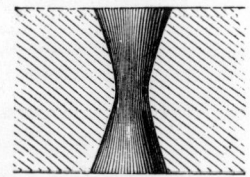

Fig. 4.—Section of a haft-hole in a stone axe.

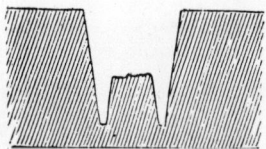

Fig. 5.—Section of a half-finished haft-hole.

times been mistaken by an unpractised eye for the petrified bone of some animal of ancient times.

Many axes of greenstone and similar kinds of stone have a hole bored for the haft. But this is never the case with flint axes, because the hardness and brittleness of the material made boring impossible.

For a long time it was uncertain how it was possible to obtain such holes in the stone axes without a metal borer. Many regarded it as impossible, but the experiments of later years have proved its feasibility beyond a doubt. An American archæologist with a wooden stick, sand, and water, actually succeeded in boring through a stone so hard that a good penknife could not make a scratch on its surface, but only left the shining mark of the metal. The stick was pressed hard against the

FIG 6.—Axe-head of greenstone, with hole partly bored. Boh. ½.

FIG. 7.—Flint arrow-head. Sk. ¼.

FIG. 8.—Small gouge, polished. Smål. ½.

FIG. 9.—Unpolished flint-axe. Sk. ⅓.

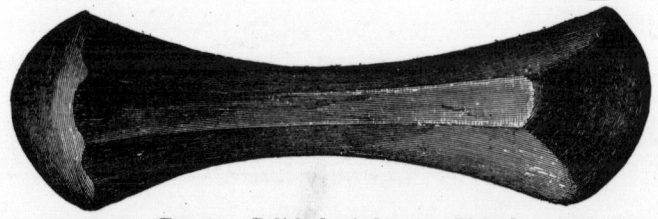

FIG. 10.—Polished grindstone. Blek. ⅓.

I.] THE STONE AGE. 15

FIG. 12.—Flint-scraper. Sk. ½.

FIG. 11.—Flint spear-head. V.-Götl. ½.

FIG. 13.—Flint knife. Sk. ⅔.

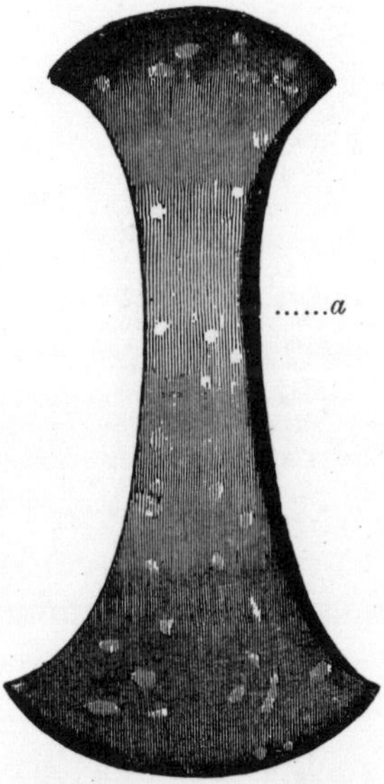

FIG. 14.—Stone axe with haft-hole (*a*). Sk. ½.

FIG. 15.—Lunate flint saw. Bohusl. ½.

stone, and was continually turned round with great rapidity. In this way the grains of sand were forced into the lower end of the stick, and by slow degrees wore a hole in the stone. The boring was begun from both sides of the stone. At first holes were formed on either side, which, as the boring continued, tapered more and more to a point. When at last the thin wall which divided them was broken through, they were like two cones placed point to point. Among the stone axes found in Sweden there are many with their haft holes unfinished. In their different degrees of completion they represent exactly the several stages in the work of boring just described (see Fig. 4).

Other stone axes with unfinished haft-holes found in Sweden seem however to have been bored in a different manner. In the middle of the hole is left a round "core," so to speak, of stone tapering upwards, as seen in the transverse section in Fig. 5. It was long supposed that such a hole must have been produced with a cylindrical metal borer; but Professor Keller at Zurich, celebrated for his excellent work on the Swiss lake-dwellings, bored similar holes in some stone axes though using only sand, water, and a hollow bone, or a cylinder of horn or wood. The hole so bored had, before it was completed, an appearance exactly like that seen in Fig. 6. Even in this case it was of course the sand which really produced the hole. This method is far less tedious than the first, because it is not necessary to rub away all the stone out of the hole, but only the ring round the central projection.

All this shows that the ancient implements of the Stone Age found in Sweden were, almost without an exception, made in that country. Besides this, several places have been discovered in Sweden where the manufacture of flint implements during this Age took place. These places are covered with a number of flint chips, works which are half-prepared or which have been damaged in making, chipping-stones, grind-stones, and the like. Such "workshops" are found in the south as far north as Bohuslän, but mostly in Skåne, where good flint is easily procured.

The Northmen of the later Stone Age had raised themselves so much above the state of savages, that they not only made such objects as were indispens-able for the necessaries of life, but took no little pains to have them as ornamental as possible. We see this, not to mention other proofs, in the fact that the axes and chisels are usually carefully ground not only at the edge, but over the whole surface (Figs. 8, 19). We have a beau-tiful example of the taste shown by the people of the Stone Age in the flint dagger de-scribed in Fig. 16 and many other objects of a similar kind.

FIG. 16.—Flint dagger. Sk. ½.

The long, narrow spearheads of flint bear witness to the extraordinary skill with which the flint was worked;

especially when we consider that they were not deliberately ground, but chipped with a boldness which was only surpassed by the accuracy with which the blows with the stone hammer were made. The least false stroke or the slightest shake of the hand would have sufficed to destroy the whole work—work which our own age, with its skill so highly developed in many other ways, would be unable to produce.

The character of the dwellings during the Stone Age is not at present known, nor can it be certainly proved by anything yet discovered. But we may well conjecture that they were either tents made of hides, like the Lap huts, or simple hovels built of wood, stones and turf. The ruins of the lake-dwellings of Switzerland show that in that country the homes of the Stone Age were wooden huts.

Professor Nilsson has called attention to the undeniable resemblance in form between the Scandinavian passage-graves and the homes of the Arctic races in America and Europe (See Fig. 17, and comp. Fig. 33). He believes that these passage graves, which as graves have a very unsuitable and unnatural form, were made after the pattern of the homes of the living people, and so accounts for their resemblance to the homes still found in the Arctic regions. If so, these early dwellings were formed of a low, quadrilateral, oval, or round room, which was approached from the south or east by a still lower long and narrow passage.

The only certain remains however of the Northern homesteads of this age, hitherto discovered, are the fireplaces, which are found in the "kitchen-middens" and in several other places. Such simple fireplaces, formed of loose stones piled together, and now become brittle from the action of fire, and begrimed with soot and ashes, are found in several places in the south of Sweden, under conditions which show that they belong to the later Stone Age.

The tools with which the Northmen during the Stone

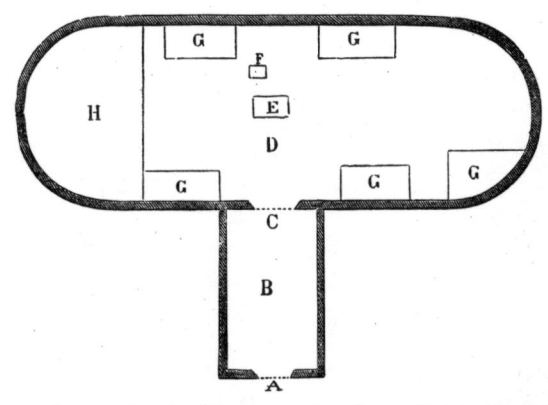

FIG. 17.[1]—Plan of a Lap dwelling (*gamme*) at Komagfjord in North Finmark, near Hammerfest.

Age produced their wooden works, were mainly knives, saws, borers, chisels, and axes or hatchets.

For knives they used flakes of flint like that described in Fig. 13. These have on either hand, when well wrought and uninjured, a very sharp edge which was not produced by grinding, but is due to the sharp angle at which the surfaces meet. Flint knives, like that in

[1] The greatest height of the room here figured was 5 ft. 10 in. (near point F), the breadth 13 ft. 8 in., and the whole length 29 ft. A represents the outer door; B the passage, 3 ft. high, 5 ft. 10 in. broad, and 11 ft. 5 in. long; C the inner door opening into the room D; E the fireplace, formed of a few large stones laid on the bare ground; F an opening in the roof to let out the smoke; G G sleeping places; and H a part of the room partitioned off for the sheep and goats.

20 ANCIENT SWEDISH CIVILISATION. [CHAP.

Fig. 16, could not have been used for cutting wood—they were either hunting-knives or daggers.

The flint tools of a lunate form appear to have been used as saws, and their edge is often very distinctly serrated, as in Fig. 15.

The edge of the chisels is either flat or hollow; of the latter—gouges as we should call them—we have an example in Fig. 8. It is about as large and broad as those we now generally use; but most of the stone chisels are larger and broader.

The axes or hatchets were not uncommonly very large (see Figs. 6, 9, 19); those of flint sometimes as much as

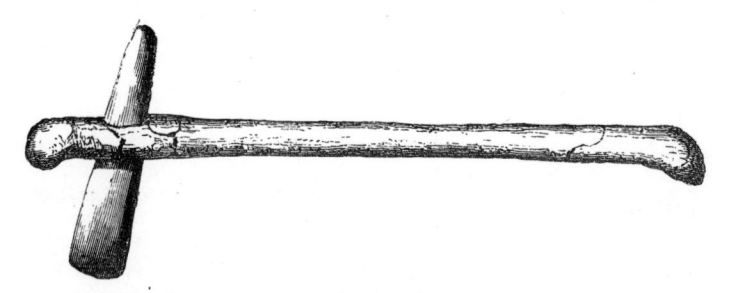

FIG. 18.—Stone axe with wooden handle found in an English bog.

eighteen inches long. It is easy to see how the hafts were fitted into the pierced stone axes. But the flint axes, as we said above, are never perforated. In most cases their hafts were probably fastened in the manner shown in Fig. 18, which represents a stone axe found in an English peat bog with the handle still preserved. A flint axe found in a peat bog at Borreby, in Skåne, has still marks which show that it was hafted in the same way (Fig. 19). Besides the stone axes with handles preserved, sometimes found in Europe, axes have also been brought home in later times from the wild peoples

I.]   THE STONE AGE.   21

of the New World, which show how such implements could have handles securely fastened without a hole (Fig. 20).

That it was possible to produce very fine works with what seem such simple stone tools, is shown both from our

Fig. 20.—Stone axe with wooden handle, from New Caledonia.

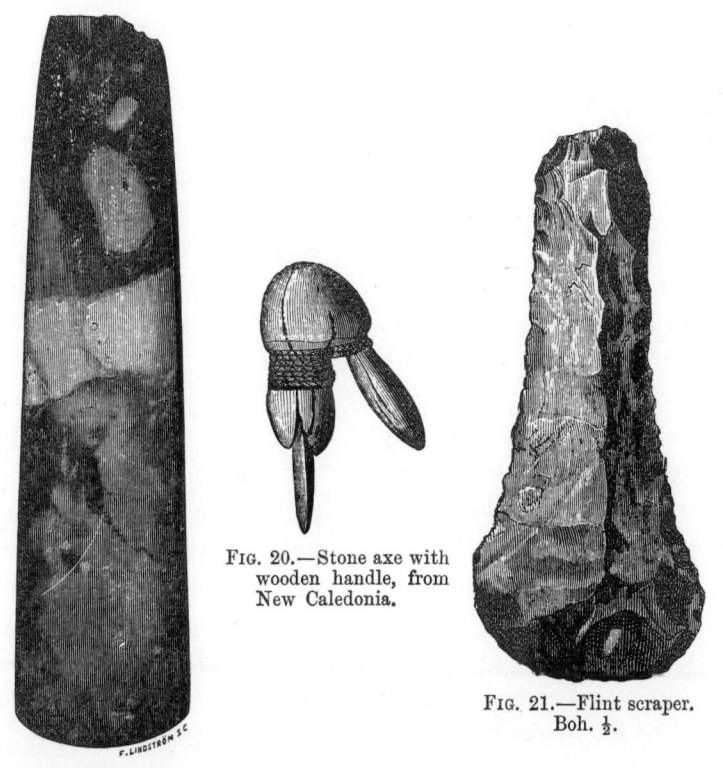

Fig. 21.—Flint scraper. Boh. ½.

Fig. 19.—Flint axe showing marks where the haft was fastened. Sk. ⅓.

experience of the Stone Age peoples of the New World, and from the often beautifully executed implements of bone, horn, amber, and the like, which are found in the "kitchen-middens" and the passage-graves (see for example Figs. 24, 25, 26, and *Ant. suéd.*, Figs. 53, 75—91). This fact has also been fully confirmed by experiments. In Denmark Chamberlain Sehested lately had some trees felled, and all the work necessary for building a small house, with both windows and doors, carried out with nothing more than axes and other implements of flint; no metal tool was allowed to be used.

Among the implements employed during the Stone Age in making clothes, we may mention especially a number of flint scrapers (Figs. 12, 21) with which the hides to be used for the purpose were cleaned and prepared; we find also awls, needles, and a comblike apparatus of bone. The last was probably used, just as instruments of the kind are by the Eskimos, in cutting out the leather threads for sewing.

No remains of clothes have as yet, it is true, been discovered in the finds of the Stone Age made in the North; still there is good reason to suppose that they were for the most part, if not exclusively, made of skins and hides, as is still the case with the most northerly peoples of Europe and America. It is however possible that towards the close of that period woven stuffs of wool were known in Northern countries, because the sheep at that time occurs as a domestic animal. The remarkable finds in the Swiss lake dwellings, so instructive as illustrating the condition of ancient peoples, have shown that during the Stone Age in Switzerland not only woven stuffs were known, but that flax even was cultivated in those times.

The amber, which occurs in large quantities upon the south coasts of Scandinavia, and especially on those of Jutland, was used even during the Stone Age for ornaments, such as beads and the like, which were worn as necklaces. Fig. 24 shows us a bead of the form which was usual at this time, but is hardly ever met with in finds of a later date. In Swedish graves amber beads are found, often in great numbers, and that not only in Skåne, but also in Vester-Götland, whither the amber must have been brought from Skåne or Denmark, a long distance for those times. For instance, more than two hundred amber beads were found in a passage-grave near Falköping in 1868.

Besides these there have been found in similar graves beads and pendants made of bone, and perforated teeth of bears, wolves, dogs, and other animals; they were evidently once used as ornaments. The teeth of the large forest animals were also worn as tokens of victory, as proud mementoes of a strife which was attended with far greater danger to the huntsmen of the Stone Age than to our modern sportsmen armed with rifles. The custom of wearing the perforated teeth of animals as ornaments survived the Stone Age. Even at the present day it exists among several peoples.

Shields were probably the only defensive weapons during this Age; but being of course made entirely of wood, leather, and other perishable materials, we have no remains of them preserved.

The offensive weapons were battle-axes and hammers, daggers, spears or lances, bows and arrows, and probably also clubs and slings. The last two are very common among wild peoples, but, for the same reason as the shields, have perished without a trace. The other classes of weapons however have been preserved by thousands to our own time.

We ought no doubt to regard as weapons stone axes, like those represented in Figs. 14 and 22; while most

24   ANCIENT SWEDISH CIVILISATION.   [CHAP.

of the other axes of flint and greenstone described above (Figs. 6, 9, and 19) were certainly used both as tools and weapons.

In Fig. 16 we have a dagger beautifully executed. The handle is broadened out away from the blade, and

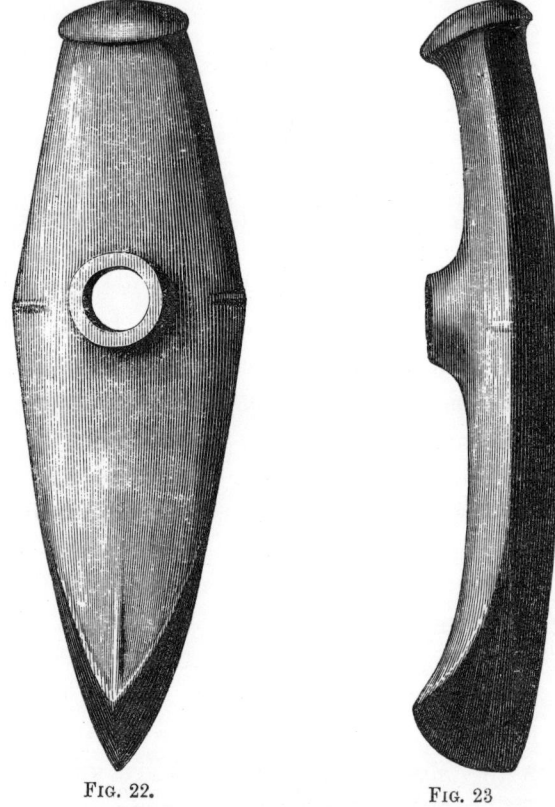

FIG. 22.   FIG. 23
Stone axe with haft-hole. Sk. ½.

has very delicate and regular nicks along the edges. The spear-heads and arrow-heads were usually made of flint, sometimes of bone. Even the latter were often provided, as Fig. 25 shows, with thin sharp flakes of flint introduced into the furrowed grooves on the sides. The flint spear-head represented in Fig. 11 in half its natural size, was found in a passage-grave near

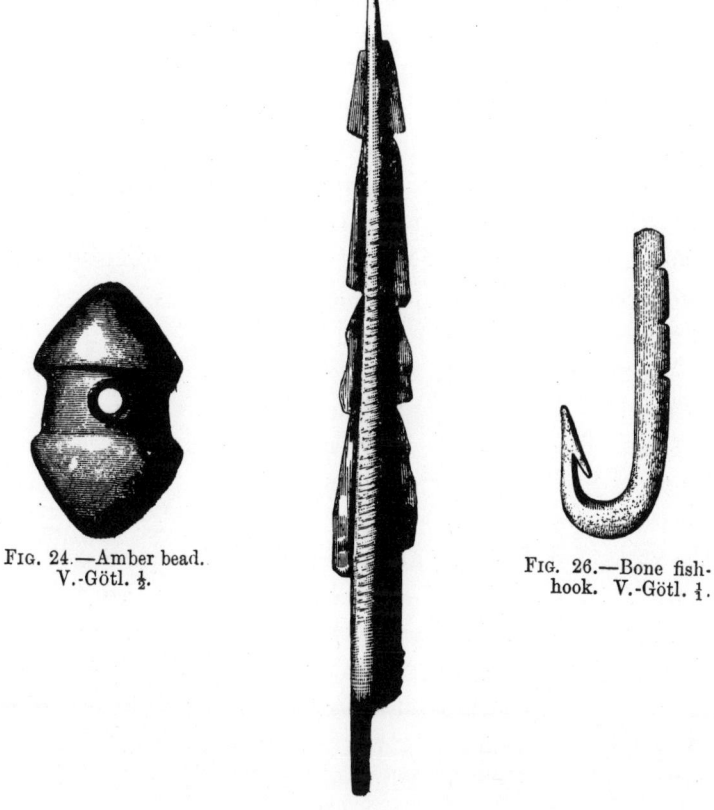

FIG. 24.—Amber bead. V.-Götl. ½.

FIG. 25.—Bone arrow-head with flakes of flint let in on the sides. Sk. ½.

FIG. 26.—Bone fish-hook. V.-Götl. ¼.

Falköping in Vester-Götland. Others are much larger, some being as much as fifteen inches long. Most of the flint arrow-heads are either long, narrow and three-sided, or short, broad, and thin; the latter are usually barbed (see Fig. 7). Besides these a kind of chisel-edged flint arrow-head has been sometimes found (see *Ant. suéd.*, Fig. 66). A large number of these were discovered on what is known as Lindormabacken, a sand-field upon the coast south of Kristianstad, where the work of making flint implements was carried on on a large scale during the Stone Age. A chisel-edged arrow-head was found still fixed in the shaft in a Danish peat-bog; and in a cave in France, which was used as a grave-chamber—probably in the later Stone Age—several human skeletons were discovered in 1871, one of them being that of a man who had been killed by an arrow of the sort described. The arrow still remained deeply rooted in one of the vertebræ.

We have also other examples of men killed by stone weapons. In the beginning of this century a stone cist was discovered in the bottom of a cairn in the south of Scotland. It contained the skeleton of a man who had one arm all but severed from the shoulder by the stroke of a stone axe; a piece of the axe still remained in the bone. Also in a grave at Borreby in Denmark a small flint arrow-head was found sticking in the eyehole of a skull. That these weapons were used in the chase as well as in warfare is not only probable in itself, but is actually proved by the occasional discovery of the bones of animals which had been wounded or killed by stone weapons. For example the skeleton of a stag was found some years ago in Denmark, which had a flint arrow-head sticking in its cheek-bone.

Fishing and the chase supplied the chief means of subsistence during the Stone Age, and indeed, as the "kitchen-middens" show, the sole means during the earlier part of the period. Probably the larger animals were often caught and killed in holes or pitfalls, in the same way as in other countries and in later times.

We have traces of fishing in Sweden during the Stone Age in the hooks which have been found made either entirely of bone (Fig. 26), or of bone with the point and barb of flint, besides harpoons and fishing-spears, the latter of bone. Nets and seines were probably not unknown. Among the relics of the lake dwelling at Robenhausen in Switzerland, belonging to this Age, a piece of net was found with nearly two-inch meshes.

That the inhabitants of the North, even during the earlier Stone Age, had some kinds of boats or ships for

FIG. 27.—Stone handmill. V.-Götl. ⅛.

fishing and sea-faring is proved, among other things, by the discovery in the "kitchen-middens" of such kinds of fish as could only have been caught in the deep-sea water. The oldest boats were probably made of the hollowed trunks of trees, such as are sometimes met with in our bogs and lakes: though none of those now known can be referred to the Stone Age. A few boats of the kind however were found in the lake-dwelling at Robenhausen just mentioned; and the South Sea Islanders knew how to make such boats—"canoes" as they call them—long before they got the knowledge of metals from the Europeans.

The bones of domestic animals found in passage-graves of Vester-Götland—namely, cattle, horses, sheep, goats (?), and pigs—show that the inhabitants of Sweden during the last part of the Stone Age were not entirely dependent for their subsistence on the proceeds of fishing and the chase. In Switzerland we find that during this period not only was pasturage regularly carried on, but that even tillage was already practised in that country. Besides flax, which we have already mentioned, they grew several kinds of corn (three sorts

FIG. 28.—South-African handmill in use.

of wheat, as well as two-cornered and six-cornered barley). We have no direct proof of tillage in Sweden during the Stone Age, but there are facts which have long been thought to show that it was even then not altogether unknown in that country. This view has lately been confirmed by the discovery of a stone handmill belonging to this period (Fig. 27). Mills of the kind are still in vogue among certain peoples, and in Fig. 28 we see how they were used.

The fireplaces already mentioned[1] show that the

[1] P. 8.

inhabitants of the North during the Stone Age cooked their food. They might have got fire either by rubbing together two perfectly dry sticks with great rapidity for a long time, as is still done by many wild peoples, or by the help of flint and pyrites used in much the same way as flint and steel. In English graves flints and pieces of pyrites have been found together bearing evident traces of having been used for this purpose.

FIG. 29.—Clay hanging-cauldron. Sk. ½.

Many of the earthenware vessels which have been found in Swedish graves were no doubt used as cauldrons for cooking. Several of them have on their sides small holes, which seem to show that the vessel was hung up over the fire (Fig. 29, cf. *Ant. suéd.*, Fig. 94). They

FIG. 30.—Animal figure on a horn axe. Sk. ¼.

are often very well made, although they were evidently formed with the hand merely, without the help of a potter's wheel. They are not unfrequently decorated with punched ornaments filled with a white material, probably chalk.

From the earthenware vessels we learn the character of the ornamentation during the Stone Age. The decorations consist only of straight lines; as yet we find neither spirals nor other ornaments with curved lines. On a horn axe (*Ant. suéd.*, Fig. 43), which probably belongs to an early part of this period, we see two very well engraved representations of animals, one of which is given in Fig. 30.

The inhabitants of Sweden during the Stone Age had

Fig. 31.—Dolmen at Haga, on the island of Orust. Boh.

already, in all probability, fixed dwelling-places. This appears from their often magnificent tombs, which seem to point to the beginning of an organized society and the combined industry of a small community, or of a whole tribe. The graves of this period are commonly described as "dolmens" (*stendösar*), "passage-graves" (*gånggrifter*), and "stone cists" (*hällkistor*).

A dolmen is a grave-chamber, of which the walls are formed of large thick stones set up edgewise, and reaching from the floor to the roof. On the inside they are smooth, but the outside is left rough (Fig. 31). The floor consists of sand, gravel, and the like. The roof is

Fig. 32.—Two passage-graves at Luttra. V.-Götl.

usually formed of one huge block of stone, which also is smooth on the side within the chamber, but otherwise uneven. The chamber has either four or five sides, or is oval or nearly round.

The passage-graves, or "giants'-chambers," as they are also called, are built in the same way as the dolmens, but they are larger and distinguished by an often very long covered passage leading to the east or south (Figs. 32, 33). There are several intermediate forms between these and the dolmens.

The chamber in a passage-grave is not unfrequently as much as twenty-four feet long, or more, nine feet

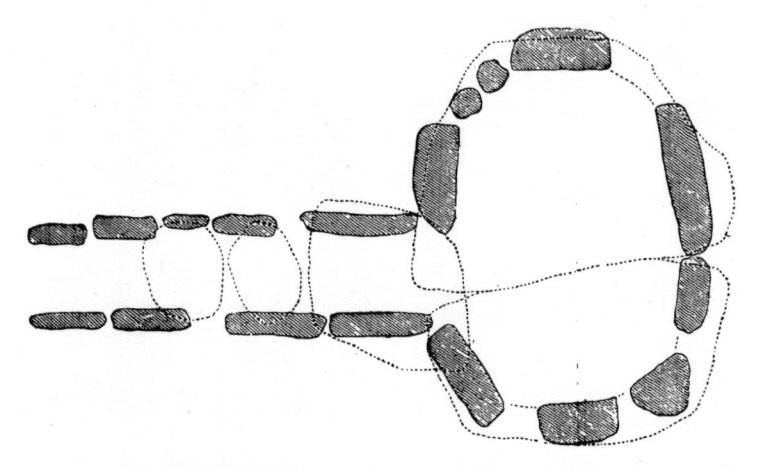

Fig. 33.—Plan of a passage-grave near Falköping. V.-Götl.

broad, and nearly six feet high. The passage is narrower and lower, but sometimes as long as the chamber.

These graves are surrounded by a low barrow, upon the top of which the roof stones of the grave-chamber were originally visible.

Dolmens and passage-graves occur in Sweden in considerable numbers along the coast of Skåne, in Skaraborgs-län, in Vester-Götland, and in Bohuslän; more sparsely, in other parts of Vester-Götland and in Halland.

Even in Nerike and West Södermanland some *tumuli* have been discovered which, in form at least, are very like the passage-graves. Not long ago a dolmen was discovered in the south-east of Norway, the first in that country. In Denmark graves of the kind are very common. They also occur in the British Isles and along the coasts of Europe from the mouth of the Vistula on to the coasts of France and Portugal, in Italy, Greece, and the

FIG. 34.—Stone cist near Skottened. V.-Götl. 21 ft. long.

Crimea, and also in North Africa, Palestine, and India. All however do not belong to the Stone Age. The Khási, a wild people dwelling on the highland of India, even at the present day still construct a sort of dolmen, in which they bury their dead.

A stone cist is a large, oblong, and four-sided grave; in point of size and construction it is much like the chamber of a passage-grave, except that it has no passage, and is usually built of thinner stones. The lower part is surrounded by a small barrow of earth or stones, but the upper part is often bare (Fig. 34). These graves are highly interesting as representing an intermediate form between the passage-graves and the great stone cists of the early Bronze Age, which are entirely covered with a barrow.

Stone cists standing free with the upper part

FIG. 35.—Stone cist near Karleby. V.-Götl. 23 ft. long.

visible over the surrounding barrow, a form of grave peculiar to Sweden, occur in great numbers in Vester-Götland, Bohuslän, Dalsland, and the south-west of Vermland. On the island of Öland also a few graves have been discovered which must be referred to this class. Stone cists entirely covered with a barrow (Figs.

35, 36) are found in the same provinces, as well as in Nerike, Öster-Götland, Småland, Bleking, and the island of Gotland.

Of the forms of graves which we have described the dolmens have proved to be the earliest; the passage-graves are a little later; the uncovered stone cists are later still; while the cists covered with a barrow belong to the time of transition between the Stone and

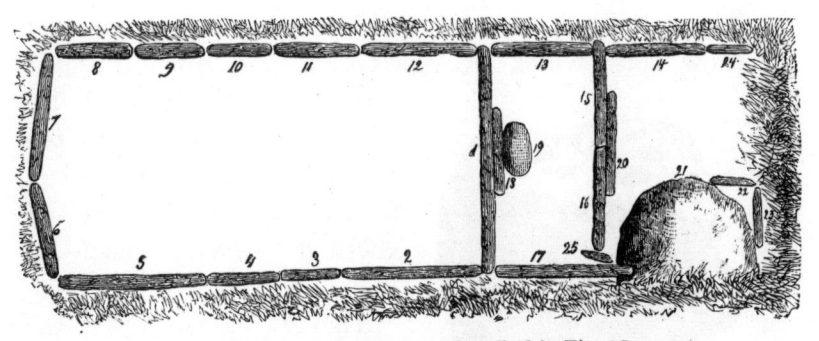

Fig. 36.—Plan of the stone cist described in Fig. 35.

Bronze Ages. The last resemble very closely the graves of the first part of the Bronze Age.

During the Stone Age bodies were always buried unburnt, in a recumbent or sitting position. Many passage-graves contain from fifty to a hundred bodies. By the side of the dead body was usually laid a weapon, a tool, or some ornaments. We often find in graves of this period earthenware vessels, now filled only with earth. Possibly they once contained food, which the dead, it was supposed, might need in the life beyond the grave. The care bestowed upon the last resting-place of the departed certainly betokens a belief in a future life; but the things placed by the side of the dead seem to show that that life was believed to be merely a continuation of the life on earth, with the same needs and the same pleasures.

Upon the upper surface of the roof-stones of graves belonging to the Stone Age are often seen small, round, sometimes oblong, cup-shaped depressions. These were certainly used for offerings either to or for the dead. In Fig. 37 we see a sacrificial stone of this sort, which was found a little while ago in the passage to a passage-grave. What gives us good ground to suppose that these holes, which are now popularly called "elf-mills," were actually intended for offerings, is that even to the present day they are in many places regarded as holy, and offerings secretly made in them.

FIG. 37.—Offering-stone. V.-Götl.

The graves show that the greater part of the present Götaland, the South of Vermland, as well as Nerike and West Södermanland were more or less thickly populated before the end of the Stone Age. Even in other parts of the country—especially East Södermanland, Upland, and Vestmanland—stone implements have been met with here and there; but it would be difficult to say how far they should be regarded as relics of the Stone Age, or as belonging to a somewhat later time. For stone implements were still used during the Bronze Age, as we see from many finds.

Of all the Swedish provinces Skåne and especially the low land along the coast was undoubtedly the most thickly peopled. Of about 64,000 relics of stone, which are now known to have been found in **Sweden**, more than 45,000 come from Skåne. Only about 4,000 are known from the whole of Svealand and Norrland. In Skåne by far the majority of the stone implements, that is nearly 40,000, are of flint. In the Mälar Valley flint implements are so scarce that among the 1,500 stone implements from Södermanland as yet known little more than a hundred are of flint.

At the end of the Stone Age the inhabitants of the North were not only still entirely ignorant of metals— even gold, but also of the art of writing. And consequently we have no remains of the language of this age to show us what the people was which then called Sweden its fatherland. An attempt has been made to answer this question by means of the skulls found in the graves of the Stone Age. Some are very like those of the Laps, but most of them bear a close resemblance to the Swedish skulls of the present day; which seems to show that a mixture of two different races had at this very early time already taken place.

This circumstance, coupled with the fact that no considerable immigration of a new people into Sweden seems to have taken place after the end of the Stone Age, makes it highly probable that the Teutonic ancestors of the Swedes began to settle in the land from the beginning of the Later Stone Age. The smaller number of skulls of a non-Scandinavian type, which occur in the graves of the Stone Age, are, no doubt, relics of the people who dwelt in the country before the Swedish immigration.

That the Stone Age lasted for a very long time in the North is proved, among other things, by the fact that this period reached a far higher development there than anywhere else in Europe. At what time the Stone Age began in Sweden we cannot even approximately determine. But everything seems to show that it ended rather before than after 1500 B.C., and therefore about 3500 years before our time. In many countries of the

Fig. 39.—Knife of slate. Ångermanl. ½.

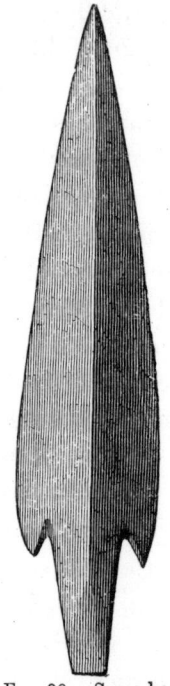

Fig. 38.—Spear-head of slate. ½.

East and in the south of Europe the Stone Age had come to an end long before; while in some parts of the New World this stage of civilisation has continued to our own day.

Besides the relics of the Stone Age already discussed, which are found almost entirely in the middle and south of Sweden, several antiquities of stone—usually of slate—have been found in the north part of the country, which do not seem to have belonged to the people who constructed the dolmens and the passage-graves. These antiquities, which are called Arctic, and of which we have specimens in Figs. 38 and 39, are chiefly met with in Lapland and Norrland, and bear a close resemblance to those which are found in Finland and other Northern countries inhabited by Laps, Fins, or other peoples closely related to them. All this seems to prove that the Arctic stone implements are relics of the Laps, and belong to the time when this people was still ignorant of the use of metal. At the same time the comparatively large number of such stone implements met with in the districts on the coast from Vesterbotten to Gestrikland, and also in Dalarna, districts not now inhabited by Laps, shows that formerly they dwelt in far more southerly tracts of Sweden than at the present day.

Relics of the Stone Age have been found in almost every country in the world, in England and in France, as well as beneath the classical soil of Italy and Greece, in Egypt, Asia Minor, and India, as well as in China and Japan.

The most important contribution to our knowledge of the Stone Age was made by the discovery of the lake-dwellings in Switzerland—in the winter of 1854-5. Since then remains of these peculiar buildings have been found in many different places, both in Switzerland and other countries. They were built up out of the water upon thousands of piles driven into the bottom of the lake. Many of these buildings had been burnt, or destroyed from some other cause, during the Stone Age; others are later. In many cases the peat formed over the ruins has preserved even the smallest and most delicate parts of their contents. These remarkable discoveries point to a people of the Stone Age with fixed dwelling places engaged in pasturage and tillage, with many other proofs of a higher culture than we are accustomed to ascribe to this period.

That a Stone Age is not necessarily accompanied by an entire want of culture, is shown also by the surprisingly high civilisation which existed in Tahiti even before the first visit of the Europeans. And yet the inhabitants of this island were so completely ignorant of metals, that at first they planted the iron needles got from Cook's people in their gardens, believing that they were shoots of some very hard plant, out of which they hoped that the life was not altogether extinct.

After the Stone Age had come to an end the true meaning of the stone implements was soon forgotten. When they were from time to time found in the ground they were called "thunder-bolts" or "Thor's bolts," and were believed to have fallen with the lightning. This belief and this name, both still very general in Sweden, are found also to a remarkable extent in all parts of the world, from Japan to South America.

Equally common with this belief of the heavenly origin of the stone axes appears to be the superstition that these "Thor's bolts" are a sovereign remedy against lightning and other disasters. Even at the present day it is often impossible to induce people to sell antiquities of stone, because they believe that by so doing they lose a protective amulet. In the museum at Visby a stone axe is preserved which was long used by its owner to hang in her vat, in order to prevent the troll from destroying the brew. And only a short while ago a peasant in

Vermland employed stone axes to sink his nets. He had observed, he fancied, that the fish went much more readily into them than into those which were not so weighted.

These old stone implements were also supposed to possess a marvellous power against sickness in men and animals. In the National Museum some stone implements are preserved, of which the edges had been chipped off and given as a medicine to sick cattle.

We know of stone implements used as amulets belonging to many different times and nations. A most interesting example of this is a little axe made of nephrite, probably from Egypt, which is covered with Gnostic formulæ. The letters are Greek, of the form used in Alexandria during the third and fourth centuries of our era.

CHAPTER II.

THE BRONZE AGE.

(*From about* 1500 *to* 500 B.C.)

BEFORE the Stone Age ended the inhabitants of Sweden had raised themselves considerably above the savage state; but, so long as they were completely ignorant of metals, it was impossible for them to reach a higher degree of civilisation. But at last the fruits of the civilisation attained by the cultured races of the East spread to the distant regions of the North; and through the knowledge of metals, at first only bronze and gold, there began for those lands a new era known as the Bronze Age.

By these words is understood that period in the earliest civilisation of the Northern races, when they made their weapons, tools, &c. of bronze, a mixture of copper and tin. Besides bronze, they knew only of one metal, namely, gold. Iron, steel, silver, and all other metals were still completely unknown in these countries.

Before we go further we must call attention to the inaccuracy of an opinion which not unfrequently finds expression, that all antiquities of bronze should be referred by antiquarians to the Bronze Age. Vessels, rings, buckles, needles and the like were, as we might have supposed, still made of bronze after the end of this period, just as they are even in our own day, but generally of a somewhat different composition from that used in the Bronze Age.[1] To this age belong only weapons and edge-tools made of bronze, and such vessels and ornaments as are usually found with them.

With respect to the important question *how* the Bronze Age began in the North, different opinions have been expressed. Some have supposed that it was due to the immigration of a Celtic race, others to a Teutonic immigration. Professor Nilsson has endeavoured to show that the North is indebted to Phœnician colonists for the earliest knowledge of metals, while Herr Wiberg, in Gefle, regarded the Bronze Age to have begun in the North through the influence of the Etruscans. Also Professor Lindenschmit of Mainz, who does not believe in the existence of a Bronze Age in the sense understood by the Northern antiquarians, considers that most of the bronze works in question were Etruscan.

It seems to us that there are strong grounds for the opinion that the beginning of the Bronze Age in Scandinavia was not connected with any great immigration of a new race, but that the people of the North learnt the art of working bronze by intercourse with other nations. The resemblance of the graves during the last part of the Stone Age and the early part of the Bronze Age, as well as other circumstances, point to such a conclusion. From Asia the "Bronze Culture," if we may so express the higher civilisation dependent on the knowledge of

---

[1] [The word bronze is throughout this translation, as in Swedish, used of all combinations of copper with tin or zinc, such as we commonly distinguish by the names bronze, gun-metal, bell-metal, brass, &c.—Tr.]

44 ANCIENT SWEDISH CIVILISATION. [CHAP.

Fig. 42.—Handle of dagger (Fig. 41) as seen from the top. ⅔.

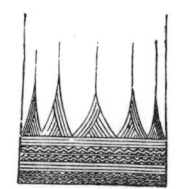

Fig. 43.—Lower part of the ferrule of a bronze spear-head. Upl. ¼.

Fig. 40.—Massive bronze axe with haft-hole. Sk. ½.

Fig. 41.—Bronze dagger with handle of the same material. Öl. ⅓.

Fig. 44.—*Fibula* of bronze. Sk. ⅔.

SWEDISH ANTIQUITIES FROM THE EARLIER BRONZE AGE.

THE BRONZE AGE.

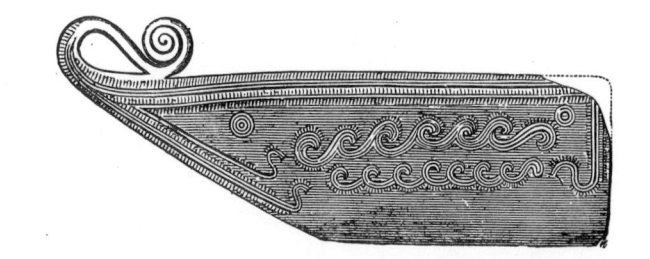

FIG. 45.—Bronze knife. Sk. ⅔.

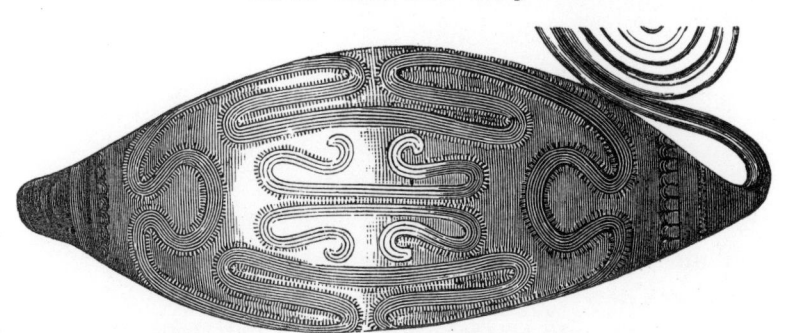

FIG. 46.—End of a large bronze collar. Småĺ. ⅔.

FIG. 47.—Upper part of the blade of a bronze sword. Sk. ⅔.

FIG. 48.—Part of the bottom of a golden bowl. (Comp. Fig. 95.) Hall. ¾.

SWEDISH ANTIQUITIES FROM THE LATER BRONZE AGE.

bronze, had gradually spread itself over the continent of Europe in a northerly and north-westerly direction, until at last it reached the coasts of the Baltic.

We have already mentioned that the end of the Stone Age, and therefore the beginning of the Bronze Age, in the North, must be regarded as having taken place 3,500 years ago. The latest investigations have shown that the Bronze Age proper came to an end in these regions in the beginning of the fifth century B.C. It lasted therefore about a thousand years.

As the Bronze Age comprises so long a period, attempts have naturally been made to distinguish the antiquities belonging to its earlier and later parts. Such attempts might have been supposed almost useless, when we consider that among the thousand of finds of the Bronze Age in the North as yet known, there is not a single coin, or any other object, with an inscription, either native or foreign. Nevertheless, by a careful and thorough examination of the many antiquities and graves of the Bronze Age now known, it has fortunately proved possible to distinguish in it six consecutive periods.[1] But as it would take us too long to describe separately each of these periods, we must restrict ourselves to mentioning which of the antiquities belong to the earlier, and which to the later, portion of the Bronze Age.

The works of the earlier part—the Earlier Bronze Age as it is called—are decorated with fine spiral ornaments and zigzag lines, as we see in Figs. 40—44. The graves generally contain remains of unburnt bodies. The antiquities of this period found in the North (which

[1] Montelius. *Om tidsbestämning inom bronsåldern med särskildt afseende på Skandinavien* (Stockholm, 1885) "The Division of Periods in the Bronze Age with special reference to Scandinavia."

appear to be almost without an exception of native workmanship) are distinguished by artistic forms, and point to a highly developed taste in the working of bronze. They generally surpass in this respect the relics of the Bronze Age found in almost all other European countries.

On the other hand a glance at Figs. 45—48 shows that the works belonging to the latter part of the period, the so-called Later Bronze Age, are characterized by a very different taste and style of ornamentation, though even they are often the result of great skill. We do not find in them spirals, of the same shape as in the Earlier Bronze Age, engraved or beaten in with a punch; but the ends of rings, knife-handles, and the like, are often rolled up in spiral volutes (Figs. 45, 46, 62). During this period the dead were always burnt.

It would take us too far a-field to discuss in full all the proofs on which the divisions of this period depends. Suffice it at present to say that such antiquities as those described in Figs. 40—44 have often been discovered in graves with unburnt bodies, but never in connexion with such articles as are represented in Figs. 45—48. These latter, on the other hand, are proved by many different finds to be contemporary with the graves which contain burnt bones. That the graves with unburnt bodies are earlier than those with burnt bones, is obvious from the fact that when, as frequently happens, both occur in the same barrow, the former are always found at the bottom, while the latter occur higher up and nearer the edges of the barrow; they must therefore have been placed there later (see Fig. 96).

By far the majority of the antiquities belonging

to the Swedish Bronze Age (of both periods) are of native production. Nearly all the articles of bronze were cast; it is only towards the close of this period that we find traces of the use of the hammer in working the bronze.

The proofs of the native origin of the antiquities of the North are partly direct, as we shall presently show, and partly only indirect. For instance, we know that most of these objects of bronze, such as we have in Figs. 40—48 and others, are of such types or forms of decoration, as are not found in any other but Northern countries. For as a rule we may safely say that if antiquities of a certain type are common within a certain district, but are not found in other parts of the world, they were made inside that district.

Sometimes we can thus see not only that a thing is native in the North, but even in what part of the North it was made. So it has often proved possible to distinguish between Swedish and Danish works of the Bronze Age. Sometimes a certain type is seen to be restricted to a still narrower compass. We have an example in the *fibulæ*, like that in Fig. 44. These occur only in the south-east of Skåne, and in the island of Bornholm; but there they are so common, that they must certainly have been made there.

The direct proofs of a considerable native manufacture of bronze objects in Sweden, during this period are, first and foremost, that several moulds have been found for the casting of axes (the so-called celts), knives, saws, and bracelets (see *Ant. suéd.*, Figs. 209—212). Such a stone mould for casting four bronze saws, which was found at Vidtsköfle, in Skåne, is represented in Fig. 49. Several other moulds intended for casting similar saws have also been discovered in Sweden and Denmark. When to this we add the circumstance that bronze saws of exactly the same form (Fig. 50) are found in great abundance in the North, but none of the sort are known from other lands, it must be allowed that

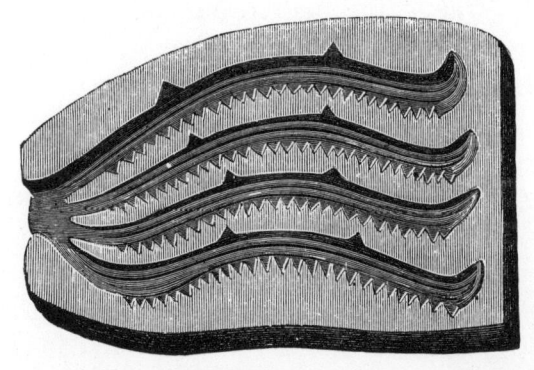

Fig. 49.—Stone mould for casting four bronze saws like that in Fig. 50. Sk. ½.

we have unusually strong evidence, both direct and indirect, that these tools originated there.

We at present know of sixteen moulds found in Sweden, and about the same number in Denmark,

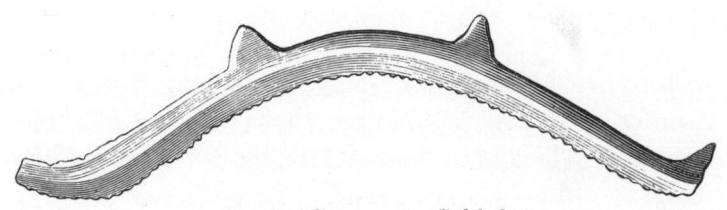

Fig. 50.—Bronze saw. Dalsl. ⅔.

belonging to the Bronze Age. The chief reason why they have not been preserved in still greater numbers, is that all the finer works in bronze were cast in a way which necessitated the immediate breaking up of the moulds.

E

The actual use of casting-moulds in the North is proved by the number of works belonging to the Bronze Age found there, which were not finished off or "planished" after casting, and so were only half-executed; as also by those which were damaged in casting. One of the most remarkable examples of the latter is a bronze vessel, found on the island of Fyen (of the same shape as in Fig. 95), which is still filled with the core, over which the thin metal was cast. The casting had miscarried, and there was a large hole on one side of the vessel.

In addition to the moulds a great many other objects of the Bronze Age have been found in the North, which furnish an equally direct proof of the native working of bronze during this period. To such belong, for example, what are technically called "runners" or "jets," such as that given in Fig. 51. When the molten bronze was poured into the mould it generally filled up also the neck or hole above, through which the metal ran. When the casting was completed and the bronze had cooled, the runner, that is the lump of bronze which remained in the hole and did not belong to the object cast, was of course broken off. The original of Fig. 51 was evidently cast in a mould the neck of which was divided into four channels, as in Fig. 49; it was found at Bräcke in Jern parish, Dalsland, near the shore of the Vener Lake. It was lying in an earthenware vessel which contained also several other runners and lumps of bronze, besides several broken pieces of swords, rings, needles,

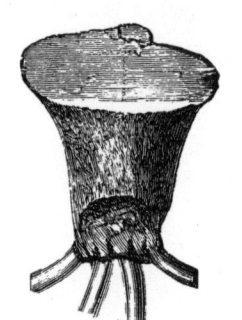

FIG. 51.—Bronze runner with four jets. Dalsl. ¼.

saws, &c., all of the same material. This discovery of a "bronze-founder's stock" gains increased interest from the fact that in the same district, at Backen in Tössö parish, a mould for casting bronze celts was also found.

Similar hoards of broken pieces of bronze works, lumps of bronze, runners, &c., evidently intended for melting down, have been often met with in other parts of the country, as at Åsled in Vester-Götland, Fredshög and Odarslöf in Skåne. Sometimes also lumps of this metal have been found in the North, whose shape seems to indicate that they have remained over in the bottom of the crucible or ladle after casting.

All the bronze used during the Bronze Age proper in Sweden is, as we said above, a compound of copper and tin, and contains usually about 90 per cent. of the former metal, and 10 per cent. of the latter. As there are no tin mines in Scandinavia, and the copper mines were probably not worked till more than a thousand years after the end of the Bronze Age, we must conclude that the bronze used during this period was imported from foreign countries. Probably it was already mixed either in the form of works, or in bars, because copper and tin in a pure state very seldom occur in the North in finds of this Age.

Almost all the bronze objects made here during the time in question were, as we have seen, cast; and the art of casting had reached an unusual degree of perfection. We have an instance of this among others in the great thin bronze vessels cast over a clay core (Fig. 95), and one still more striking in a pair of large and beautiful bronze axes with very wide spreading blades found at Skogstorp near Eskilstuna (see Fig. 52). These are not massive, but consist only of thin plates of bronze, which were cast over a still existing clay core; the bronze is hardly in any part more than the third part of a line in thickness.

We have a proof of still greater skill in casting in a sort of bronze chain sometimes found in Sweden (see Guide, Fig. 55). They are cast link within link; yet the

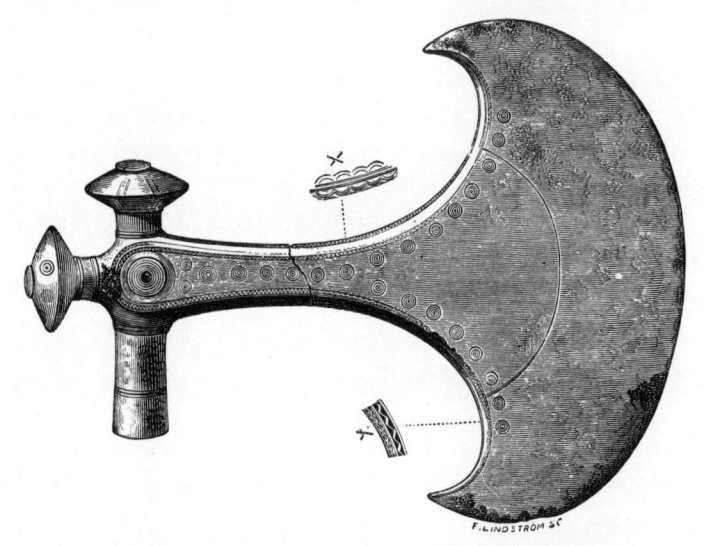

FIG. 52.—Bronze axe, of thin plates over clay core. Södermanl. ¼.

links are so tight together, that it seems scarcely possible to conceive how they could have been so cast.

The art of soldering metals was unknown in that country during the Bronze Age. When two pieces of bronze had to be joined together, or a repair was necessary, they managed it—as a number of still preserved antiquities show—either with small pins (see *Ant. suéd*, Fig. 123), or by casting bronze over the joint, often in a very clumsy way.

Buttons, sword-hilts, and other works of bronze were

sometimes decorated with pieces of amber inlaid. Still more frequently were the bronze works — hanging vessels and sword-handles, for example—decorated by inlaying a dark brown material like resin, which on the yellow bronze, almost as bright as gold, must have produced a very good effect. Large round cakes of the same material, which was also used for several other purposes of workmanship, are not unfrequently found in the peat bogs of Sweden. The largest hoard of this kind was made in the year 1845 in a small peat bog at Tågarp in Skåne, where fourteen cakes of resin were found standing edgewise close to each other. They were bored through in the middle, and had evidently been tied together. (See *Ant. suéd,* Fig. 194.)

The art of gilding, in the proper sense of the word, was certainly not yet known; but objects made of bronze are often found overlaid with thin plates of gold. We have examples of this in the two large bronze axes from Skogstorp just mentioned, as well as in several pins, buttons, sword-handles, &c.

Having thus glanced at the bronze industry in Sweden, we will endeavour to describe the most essential features of what is yet known of Northern civilisation during the Bronze Age.

Of the dwelling-houses, which were in all probability usually simple wooden huts, no traces remain, nor are there any representations of them on the " rock-carvings " (*hällristingar*). For felling trees, house-building, and other kinds of carpentry, the Northmen had during the Bronze Age nearly the same sorts of tools as we have already seen in use during the Stone Age, namely, knives, saws (Fig. 49), awls, chisels, axes and hammers;

though these tools were now more usually of bronze. But several sorts of stone tools—more particularly axes, hammers, and the like—were used even during the Bronze Age, as we know from many finds. For bronze was a costly material, and for many purposes flints or other kinds of stone, could be used with advantage.

The most common tool of the Bronze Age is a kind of axe or chisel, known by the name of "celt." These celts, which were originally copies of the stone axes, are of two kinds—the socketed celts (Fig. 58), and those which are not socketed (Figs. 56, 57). The latter were, like the flint axes, fixed into one end of a cloven haft (Fig. 53). The socketed celts, on the other hand, had a handle fixed into a socket, and bound to the little loop, which is usually to be seen just under the mouth of the socket (Fig. 54). How common both these kinds were during the Bronze Age is easily seen from the fact that, among about four thousand objects of bronze belonging to this period found in Sweden, more than one thousand are celts.

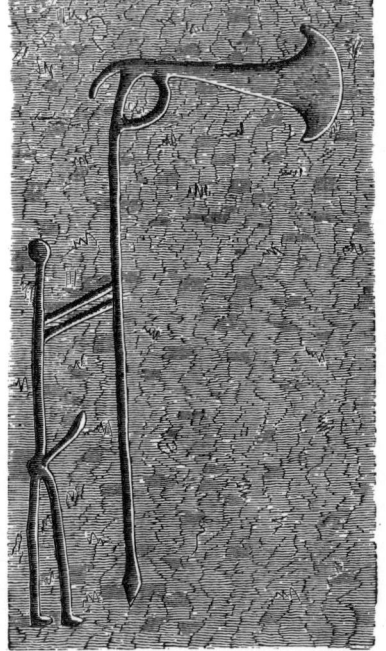

FIG. 53.—A celt (not socketed) fastened to the haft, from a rock-carving of the Bronze Age. Sk.

THE BRONZE AGE.

Similar bronze celts were used also in many other countries, both in and out of Europe (see Fig. 55), and celts of iron are still in use in Africa.

What we have already said of the other axes is equally true of the celts, that some of them were weapons, while the rest were used as tools. We ought however certainly to regard as weapons such costly and tasteful celts as that given in Fig. 57. Similar ones have often been found in graves together with other weapons.

Fig. 54.—Bronze socketed celt with wooden haft, found in a salt-mine at Hallein in Austria.

Of sewing implements there have been found especially needles, awls, tweezers, and knives. They are almost always of bronze; but a few tweezers and one awl of gold have been found in Sweden and Denmark. The awls were, of course, fixed in a haft; some hafts made of bronze, bone, and amber are still preserved. The needles were used in making woollen clothes, of which we shall speak presently. The other implements were used for sewing leather or skins. Narrow strips or threads of skin were cut out with the knife, holes

Fig. 55.—Egyptian bronze celt with wooden handle.

56   ANCIENT SWEDISH CIVILISATION.   [CHAP.

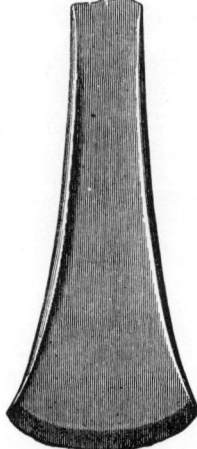

FIG. 56.—Bronze celt (not socketed). Medelp. ½.

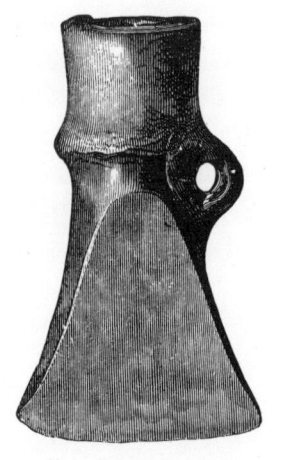

FIG. 58.—Bronze celt (socketed). Sk. ⅔.

FIG. 60.—Bronze button. Bohüs. ¼.

FIG. 57.—Bronze celt (not socketed). Öl. ½.

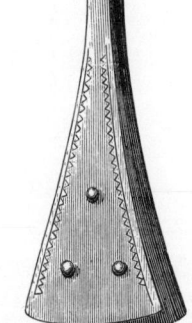

FIG. 59.—Gold tweezers. Hall. ¼.

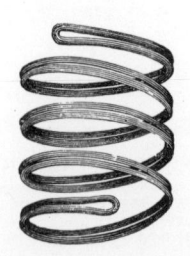

FIG. 61.—Spiral finger-ring of a double gold wire.

FIG. 62.—Gold bracelet. Sk. ¾.

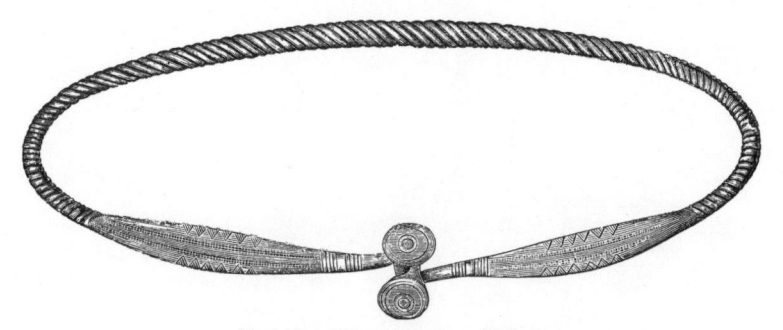

FIG. 63.—Bronze torque. Hall. ½.

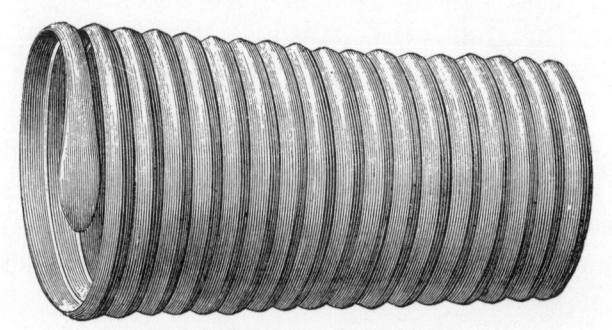

FIG. 64.—Spiral bronze bracelet. Sk. ½.

bored with the awl, and the leather thread drawn through the holes with the tweezers. These implements are much more frequent than the needles, which probably indicates that clothes of skin were far more generally worn than those of wool during this period. Scissors were unknown in the Bronze Age, but came into use in the Iron Age.

On the character of the clothes themselves light has been thrown most unexpectedly by the discoveries of

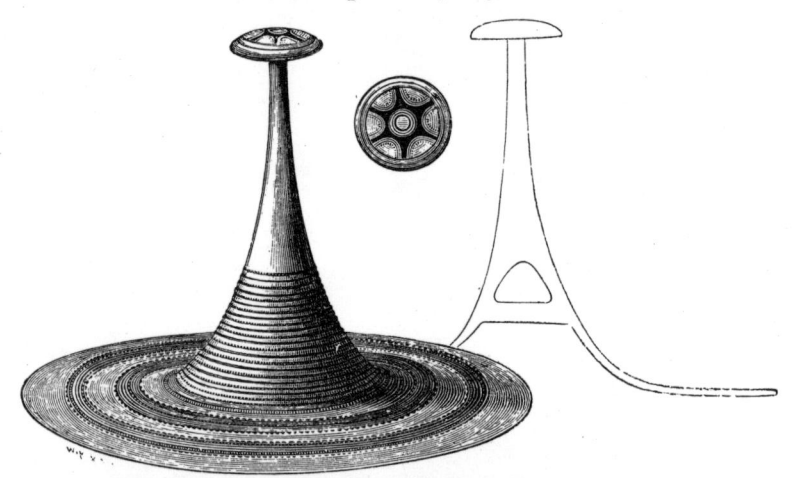

FIG. 65.—Bronze ornament with inlaid resin on the knob. Hall. ½.

late years. In the examination of a barrow at Dömmestorp, in Halland, in 1869, a piece of woollen stuff, 5 ft. long and 2 ft. wide, was found in a stone cist. It was a kind of shawl which was spread over the burnt bones deposited in the cist. The whole of it could not be recovered, but the larger pieces were secured, and are now preserved in the National Museum. The weaving is quite simple (see Fig. 66). The colour is now brown; but at both the narrower ends is seen a light yellow border, 4 in. broad.

II.] THE BRONZE AGE. 59

Still more surprising are some discoveries made in Denmark. In 1861, in the so-called "Treenhöi," a barrow at Havdrup in Ribe amt, a coffin was found made out of a cloven and hollowed trunk of an oak. In this coffin, which fortunately was examined by

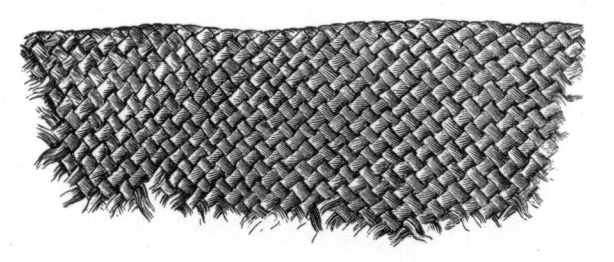

FIG. 66.—Piece of woollen stuff of the Bronze Age. Hall. ¼.

experts, a warrior had been buried with his sword and with all his clothes (Fig. 67). The still perfectly preserved clothes of simply woven wool consist of a high cap, a wide, roundly-cut mantle, a sort of tunic,

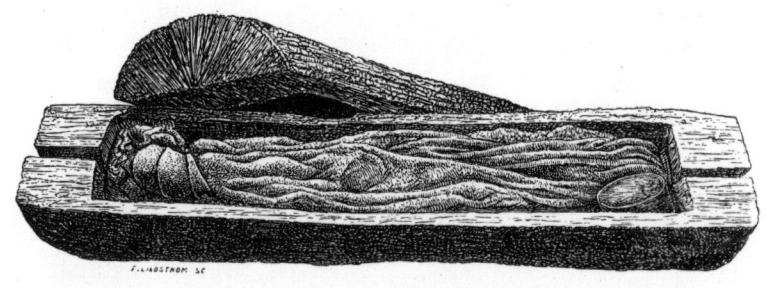

FIG. 67.—Tree-coffin of the Bronze Age, showing the body of a man wrapped in a woollen mantle, with the head towards the left. Treenhöi. Jutland.

and two small pieces of wool, which probably covered the legs; at the feet were seen some small remains of leather, which were possibly once shoes. The cap, which had no shade, was made of thick woven-wool, and the outside was covered with projecting pieces of worsted, all ending in a knot. The inside of the mantle also was covered with pendent worsted threads. The tunic was kept together by a long woollen belt, which went twice round the middle, was knotted in front, and had two long ends hanging down and decorated with fringes. They also found in the grave a second woollen cap and a woollen shawl decorated with tassels; half of the latter lay rolled up as a pillow under the head. The whole contents of the coffin were inclosed in a hide, probably that of a cow. Although the woollen clothes were so remarkably well-preserved the body had almost completely perished; even the skeleton had crumbled away. Only the black hair and the brain protected by the cap were preserved; the form of the brain could still, curiously enough, be easily recognized. By the left side of the body lay a bronze sword in a wooden sheath lined with skin. At the foot stood a round wooden box containing a smaller box of the same kind, in which lay the last-mentioned woollen cap, as well as a horn comb and a bronze knife. The knife, which in shape is like a modern razor, had possibly been used for the same purpose.

The value of this remarkable find—and others like it have since been made—is greatly increased by the discovery ten years later in 1871, of a complete woman's dress of the same period, in another Danish barrow, Borum-Eshöi, near Århus in Jutland. In this case also the body was buried in a coffin made out of a cloven and hollowed trunk of an oak. An untanned hide, probably of a cow or an ox, inclosed the contents of the coffin. The body had been wrapped in a large mantle, woven with a mixture of coarse wool and cow hair. That it was a woman who was here buried, was clearly shown by the well-preserved skeleton. The very long hair had probably been fastened up by a horn comb which was found in the grave. Upon the head was a well-knotted worsted net, which is seen at the top of Fig. 68. There were also found remains of a second similar net. The body too was clad in a complete dress of woollen stuff, consisting of a jacket with sleeves and a long robe (see Fig. 68). The weaving was of precisely the same kind as that of the clothes found in the graves of Dömmestorp and Treenhöi. The jacket was sewn together under the arms and upon the back, and open in front, where it had probably been fastened with a string or a little bronze *fibula* found in the coffin, unless the latter had been used for the mantle. The coarse seam on the back of the jacket shows that it used to be covered by the mantle.

FIG. 68.—Woman's woollen dress, from Borum-Eshöi, Jutland.

The robe was kept together round the body by two woollen bands, one of coarser, the other of finer work. The latter band, or rather belt, was of wool and cowhair mixed, woven in three rows, of which the middle appeared to have been of a different colour from those on the sides. It ended in thick ornamental tassels.

The other bronze ornaments taken out of the coffin, besides the *fibula* already mentioned, were a spiral finger-ring, two bracelets, a torque, and three round, beautifully decorated plates of different sizes with points projecting in the middle. A comparison with similar ornaments recently found in other graves proves that they were decorative plates belonging to belts. Strangely enough there lay by the side of this woman's body a bronze dagger with a horn handle.

It is difficult in most cases to decide with absolute certainty whether a grave of the Bronze Age contained the body of a man or a woman; and so we cannot adduce any other *certain* example from this period of weapons in a woman's grave. But it should be mentioned that, in a tree-coffin of oak in the so-called Dragshöi, near Ribe, a bronze dagger was found, although the long hair upon the still remarkably well preserved skull made it probable that the body there buried belonged to a woman and not to a man. Hitherto there has been a general tendency to regard each grave in which weapons are found as the grave of a man; but our experience from Borum-Eshöi shows that this view is not always correct, at least where the weapon is a dagger. No objection on the contrary can be raised against the opinion that the graves in which bronze *swords* have been found contained bodies of men.

The remarkable intimation of Amazons during the

Bronze Age in the North, which the find in Borum-Eshöi gives us, gains probability from the fact that we hear of Amazons among several peoples on the coasts of the Mediterranean, at a time when they had about the same degree of civilisation as the Northmen during the Bronze Age. We remember too the accounts of the "Shield-Virgin" even in the North during the latter part of heathen times.

We see then that the women's dress consisted during the Bronze Age of the same two most important parts—a robe and a jacket—as are now worn, at any rate in the country parts. But if the clothes found in Treenhöi ought to be regarded as an ordinary example of the men's dress of that time, it must have been very different from what is not merely now worn, but from that worn during the latter part of heathen times. The absence of breeches or trousers is particularly noticeable.

Both Treenhöi and Borum-Eshöi are proved by the bronze implements found in them to belong to a very early part of the Bronze Age, and are therefore nearly 3,000 years old. That it was possible for woollen clothes to be thus marvellously preserved in a grave for so long a time was due of course to exceptionally favourable conditions, and most particularly to the fact that they were laid in oaken coffins, the tannin in oak being remarkably conducive to the preservation of organic material.

The stuff most used during the Bronze Age was certainly wool, a native product of the sheep-farming which had been carried on in Sweden since the last part of the Stone Age. In a grave belonging to the latter part of the Bronze Age however, a piece of very fine linen was also found.

If the ornaments possessed by the Northmen during the Stone Age were insignificant, those of the Bronze Age on the contrary were far more beautiful and varied. They were chiefly made of gold and bronze. Beads and similar ornaments of amber do not appear to have been so general in the Bronze, as in the Stone

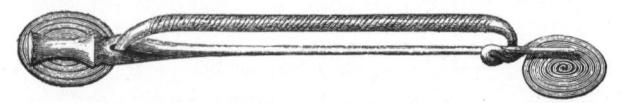

Fig. 69.—Bronze fibula. Öl. ⅔.

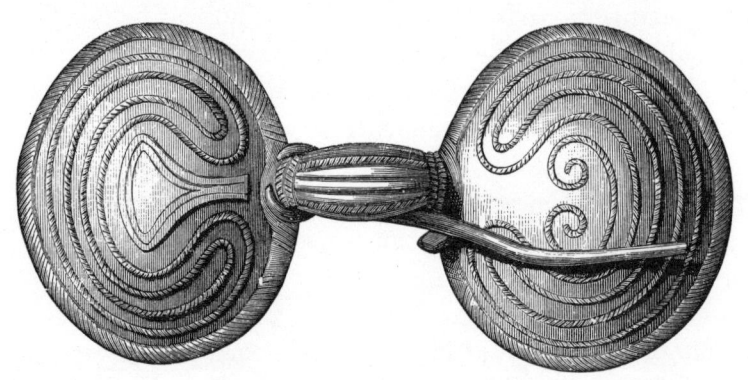

Fig. 70.—Bronze brooch. Boh. ⅔.

Age. Silver ornaments, glass beads, and the like, were still unknown.

In graves belonging to the earlier part of the Bronze Age are found beautiful ornaments for the neck and the breast (Guide, Fig. 42), *fibulæ* and brooches of bronze (Figs. 44, 69, 70), large round belt ornaments with points projecting in the middle (Fig. 65 and *Ant. suéd.* Fig. 111), bracelets and finger-rings of bronze and gold, frequently of a spiral shape (Figs. 61, 64), bronze buttons, &c. Combs, which appear to have been unknown in the

Stone Age, are not unfrequently met with in the graves of this period (Fig. 71).

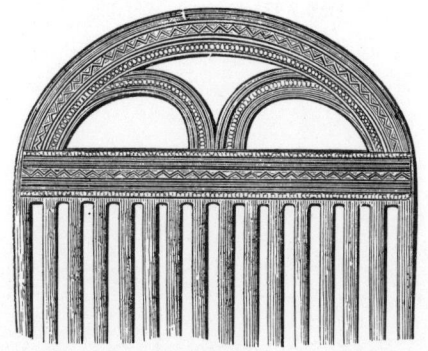

FIG. 71.—Bronze comb, with all the teeth broken off; originally they were about 1¼ inches long. Sk. ¼.

FIG. 72.—Bronze torque. Gotl. ½.

During the later part of the Bronze Age besides ornaments of the kinds already mentioned (Figs. 60, 62,

F

66 ANCIENT SWEDISH CIVILISATION. [CHAP.

70) they had also different sorts of pendants and pins (*Ant. suéd.* Figs. 213—220), and especially a great number of large bronze rings, of which the largest were worn on the neck (see Figs. 46, 63, 72, and *Ant. suéd.* Figs. 227—233). Most of these bronze rings have still

FIG. 73.—Bronze shield with *répoussé* ornaments, of foreign workmanship. Hall. ⅓.

preserved a considerable degree of elasticity, although they have lain some 2,000 years in the ground.

The weapons of the Bronze Age were to a large extent of the same kinds as those in use during the Stone Age; they consisted, namely, of daggers, axes, spears, bows and arrows, and probably clubs and slings. The most important defensive weapon was the shield, which, as we have seen, was probably used also by the people of the Stone Age. But to these were now added swords and helmets.

The shields were usually of wood or leather, but besides these some have been found in Sweden and Denmark belonging to the later part of the Bronze Age, which were entirely made of bronze. A beautiful shield of this sort, very large and almost round, consisting of a thin plate of bronze with ornaments of *répoussé* work, was found in 1865 in a peat bog at Nackhälle, near Varberg in Halland, and is now preserved in the National Museum. In the centre of the inside there is a handle, but it is so small as only to allow room for two fingers (see Fig. 73).

Only once have any traces of helmets belonging to the Bronze Age been met with, when a chin-piece beautifully decorated and overlaid with gold was found in Denmark; it belonged to the earlier part of the Bronze Age. But in the rock-carvings of the same period men are sometimes represented with helmets. No other defensive weapons, such as coats of mail and the like, have been discovered.

Swords and daggers of bronze (Figs. 41, 74) have been found in Sweden in very large numbers; more than 500 of them are already known. The swords were usually constructed for thrusting, and not for cutting, and this perhaps explains the fact, so often noticed, that the hilts of the bronze swords, especially the earlier ones, seem too short for our hands. They are generally long enough if the sword is held like a dagger. The blades are almost always two-edged and very pointed. A bronze weapon,

68   ANCIENT SWEDISH CIVILISATION.   [CHAP.

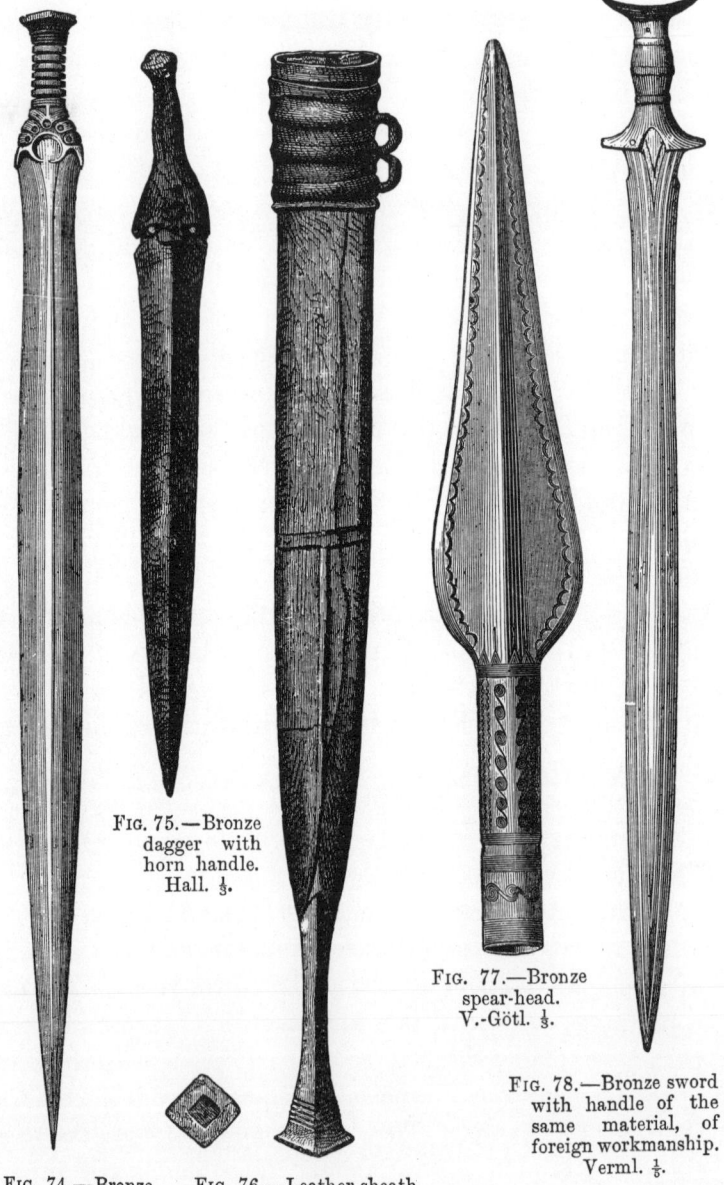

FIG. 75.—Bronze dagger with horn handle. Hall. ⅓.

FIG. 77.—Bronze spear-head. V.-Götl. ⅓.

FIG. 78.—Bronze sword with handle of the same material, of foreign workmanship. Verml. ⅕.

FIG. 74.—Bronze sword. Ö.-Götl. ¼.

FIG. 76.—Leather sheath with bronze chape for dagger (Fig. 75). ⅓.

quite unique of its kind,[1] was lately found in Öster-Götland. It has a one-edged, sabre-like blade, blunt in front and turned back at the point (see Guide, Fig. 60). The hilts which, except in the very latest, have no traces whatever of a cross-guard, were made either of bronze or of wood, bone, or horn. In the latter case they are now usually lost. The bronze hilts are often overlaid with gold and decorated with inlaid pieces of amber, or enamelled with pieces of resin in the manner above described (see p. 53).

Not unfrequently the sheaths belonging to the swords and daggers have been found in a more or less complete state of preservation. There is in the National Museum a remarkably well preserved dagger-sheath, found in 1869 at Dömmestorp in Halland, in the same grave as the remains of woollen stuff already described (see p. 58). Like many others it is made of wood overlaid with well-tanned leather, and lined with fine skin; the chape at the end is of bronze (Fig. 76). A few wooden sword-sheaths without leather have been found in Danish graves (see *e.g.* p. 60); they are sometimes decorated with carved ornaments.

Many handsome battle-axes of bronze have been found in Sweden. One, decorated with the ornamentation peculiar to the Earlier Bronze Age, is described in Fig. 40. Even many of the elegant celts (Fig. 57) were, as we have seen, undoubtedly battle-axes. The axes which we

[1] In Denmark a *flint* weapon of the same form was found, with a one-edged blade and its point bent back. This peculiar weapon must be regarded as a copy in flint of a bronze sabre like that found in Öster-Götland. In these remarkable objects belonging to an early part of the Bronze Age in the North we have undoubtedly traces of a more or less direct communication with the civilised lands of the East, where at this time weapons of a very similar form were used.

mentioned before as made of a thin plate of bronze cast over a clay core could not have been used as weapons, because they would obviously have broken to pieces with the first blow; nor could they even have been carried before some chieftain as a mark of distinction, because they are so thin and weak that they could not have stood the shaking. Possibly they were fixed as standing ornaments, perhaps in some temple.

In order to save the costly material, battle-axes of stone, and arrow-heads and spear-heads of flint were, as many finds show, still used during the Bronze Age. Archers are seen represented on the rock-carvings, but arrow-heads of bronze have very seldom been found in Sweden. It was also natural that they should prefer flint and bone for weapons so easily lost. Spear-heads of bronze are not however so rare; more than two hundred discovered in Sweden are already known (see Fig. 77, and *Ant. suéd.*, Figs. 101, 173—177). The rock-carvings show that spears were often used as missiles.

In speaking of weapons we should also mention the large and handsome war-trumpets of bronze which have been often met with, both in Sweden and Denmark (*Ant. suéd.*, Fig. 178).

Some of the weapons now mentioned, swords for example, were obviously intended exclusively for warfare; others might equally well have been used in the chase. Hunting and fishing were certainly still the most important occupations of the men in times of peace, and some bronze hooks have been found which are singularly like those in use at the present day (*Ant. suéd.*, Fig. 202).

We know that pasturage was carried on during the

THE BRONZE AGE.

Bronze Age, because we not only constantly meet with the bones of domestic animals in the finds of this period, but also sometimes come across hides of oxen and cows (both tanned and untanned), and moreover the wool so often used for clothes.

Cattle are sometimes found represented on the rock-carvings, as on one at Tegneby near Tanum church in Bohuslän. Two of the animals there represented are harnessed to a plough, which is being driven by a workman who is walking behind (Fig. 79). We have further proof that tillage was practised during this period in the bronze sickles (Fig. 80) and the hand-mills which are sometimes met with.

FIG. 79.—Plough from a rock-carving at Tegneby. Boh. $\frac{1}{20}$.

Tillage necessarily pre-supposes fixed dwelling-places; that these existed is further made probable by the

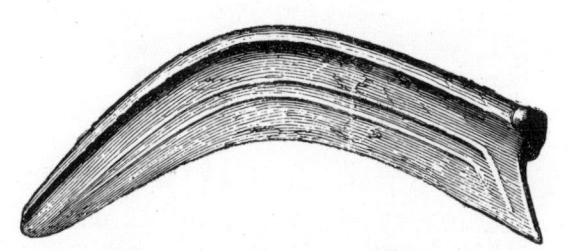

FIG. 80.—Bronze sickle. Södermanl. $\frac{1}{2}$.

fact that the barrows of this period so often lie thick together.

The rock-carvings, which throw so much light on Swedish civilisation during the Bronze Age, show that horses were already used for riding and driving. On one of the remarkable carved stones of the grave at

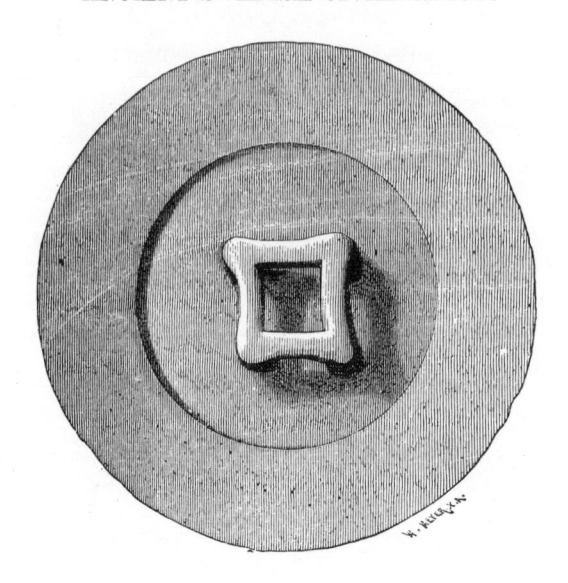

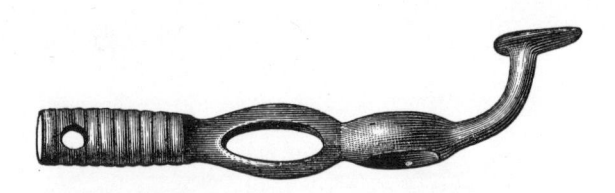

FIGS. 81-83.—Parts of a bronze set of harness.

II.] THE BRONZE AGE. 73

Kivik[1] there is a representation of a two-wheeled chariot with two horses and a driver standing upon it (Fig. 89). Figs. 81—83 represent a part of a bit and two bronze plates belonging to a set of harness which,

Fig. 84.

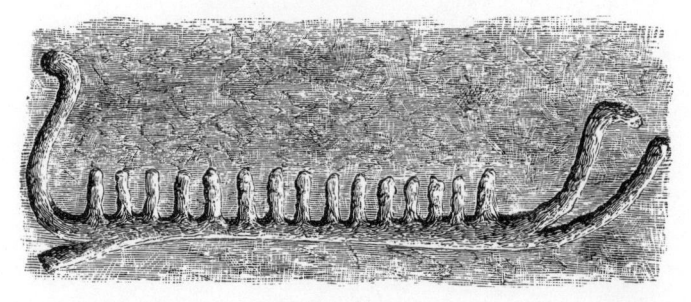

Fig. 85.

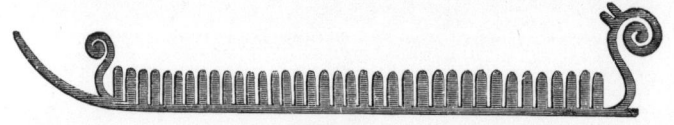

Fig. 86.

Boats from rock-carvings in Bohuslän.

together with other things of the kind, was found in Skåne. Two bronze bridles of very nearly the

[1] At the fishing village of Kivik, on the east coast of Skåne, rather more than nine miles north of Simrishamn, there is an unusually large cairn. In the middle of this, in 1750, a cist was discovered about thirteen and a-half feet long and from three to four feet broad, formed of flat stones placed edgewise. On the inside of these are several figures formed by a shallow incision of the stone, consisting of men, horses, a chariot, axes, &c.

FIG. 87.—Rock-carving near Backa. Boh.

CHAP. II.] THE BRONZE AGE. 75

same kind as those used at the present day (see Guide Fig. 68) have quite recently been discovered in Gotland in a find belonging to the last part of the Bronze Age.

It is true that in Sweden no boats have been found

FIG. 88.—Rock-carving in Lökeberg in Bohuslän.

which certainly belong to the Bronze Age; but the rock-carvings can give us some idea both of their appearance and their size, which seems to have been often very considerable (Figs. 84—88). The boats were usually unlike at the two ends, but this does not appear to have been always the case. We often see the high and narrow stem terminating in an animal's head; sometimes the stern also is similarly decorated. As no indisputable traces of masts and sails have been found on the rock-carvings, the boats of the Bronze Age would seem to have been exclusively designed for rowing. The same is also the case, as we shall presently see, with the remarkable boat found in the bog at Nydam in Denmark, which belongs to an early part of the Iron Age.

We often find sea-fights described on the rock-carvings. We have also proofs of peaceful intercourse by sea with other peoples in the many things imported from foreign lands which occur in the finds from the Bronze Age. Chief among imported goods we must reckon all the bronze used in Sweden at this time regarded as raw material. Probably also most of the gold used there during the Bronze Age was brought from other countries.

Fig. 89.—One of the stones of the grave at Kivik. Sk.

Besides these we ought also to set down as imports certain bronze works which are undoubtedly of foreign origin, because they are very rare in Scandinavia, but common in other countries. We might adduce as examples of these the bronze shield from Halland already mentioned (Fig. 73), a diminutive bronze car found at Ystad, to which we shall again presently refer (Fig. 91), some large bronze vases with embossed figures (for one

II.] THE BRONZE AGE. 77

of them see Fig. 93), some bronze swords (Fig. 78), &c. These foreign bronze works were made in Central Europe and Italy.

Writing was unknown during the Bronze Age, but there existed in Sweden during this period a sort of picture-writing preserved in the rock-carvings, which have been found most abundantly in Bohuslän and Öster-Götland, but also occur in Skåne and some other parts of Sweden (Figs. 87, 88, 89); for the latest investigations have shown that these remarkable relics belong to the time in question. One of the most important proofs of this lies in the great, and obviously not accidental, resemblance between the usual bronze swords and those frequently represented on the rock-carvings [1] (Fig. 90). The very fact of the frequent occurrence of these swords on the rock-carvings is, apart from the consideration of form, a proof that the latter cannot belong to the Stone Age, because swords were then unknown. Again that they cannot belong to the Iron Age or to any later time is proved by the fact that no explanatory notice written either in runes or any other characters has ever been found upon

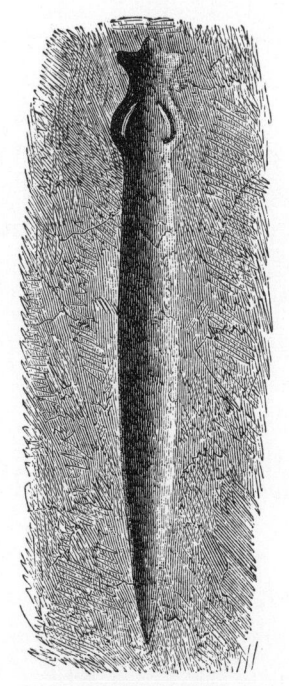

FIG. 90.—Sword on a rock-carving at Ekensberg. Ö.-Göt. $\frac{1}{16}$.

[1] This was first pointed out by the late Royal Antiquarian, Bror Emil Hildebrand.

them; the absence of anything of the kind makes it difficult to suppose that they were cut by a people who had any knowledge of writing. And the runes were known, as we shall presently see, during a great part of the Iron Age. Besides, it should be borne in mind that one of the oldest runic stones in the North was lately found in Tanum parish in North Bohuslän, a district where rock-carvings are more numerous perhaps than in any other part of Sweden.

The Northmen of the Bronze Age thus understood, by a kind of picture-writing, how to preserve the memory of important events. This circumstance gains additional weight from the fact that the Aztecs in Mexico (who, in spite of their high civilisation, were on the arrival of Cortez completely in their Bronze Age) possessed a picture-writing, but were not acquainted with an alphabet. In Sweden, as in Mexico, there certainly once existed an oral tradition necessary for its interpretation. As, however, this tradition has long died out, there is little hope that any one will be able to explain the dark speech of our "hill-pictures."

The pictures represented on these rock-carvings do not certainly point to a very high development of artistic power. But in order to form a just estimate of them we must take into account the difficulty of producing better figures upon the hard and not very smooth surface of the rock.

The Northmen of the Bronze Age also attempted to represent living objects in metal work. We have examples of this in the heads of animals with which knife handles and other bronze implements often terminated, and with which the handles of golden bowls were also similarly decorated. We moreover find a

II.]   THE BRONZE AGE.   79

few knife handles terminating in human figures. A bronze knife of this last kind was recently found in Skåne (see Guide, Fig. 52).

Considering that there are no written sources, native or foreign, from which to learn anything of the Bronze Age in Sweden, and that the tradition of the existence

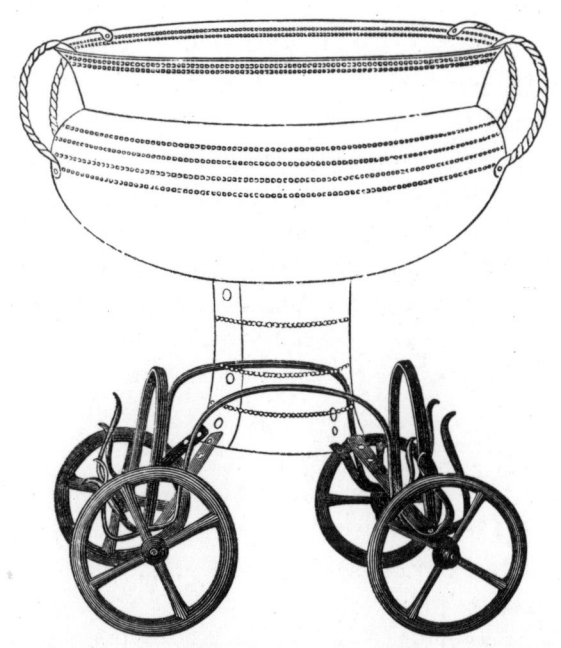

FIG. 91.—Diminutive car which probably once carried a sacrificial vessel as here traced. Sk. ¼.

of such a time has been forgotten, we can hardly expect to get much light thrown on the religion, social condition, or the manners and customs of that time. Some things have been found however which were certainly used for religious worship in that Age. One of the most remarkable of these is the little bronze car resting on four wheels, which was found in 1855 in a peat-bog at Ystad, and is now preserved in the National Museum (see Fig. 91). This car formerly carried a large bowl of bronze, as is proved by the still visible rivet holes and a comparison with a very similar car found at Peccatel in Mecklenburg. That these vessels had a religious use would be antecedently probable from the apparent resemblance between them and the great bronze cars with the laver resting upon them, which Solomon ordered to be set up in the forecourt of the Temple at Jerusalem. This view is further confirmed by the remarkable surroundings in which the Mecklenburg car was found. At Peccatel, near Schwerin, there lie, or lay then, three large barrows very close to one another. In the first of these the car was found together with various other antiquities from the Bronze Age. One of the other barrows contained a grave with burnt bones, and also a four-sided altar composed of earth and stone, about five feet high. Built up in this was a large round vessel of earthenware. By the side of the altar a human skeleton lay extended in a sort of low cist of baked clay, like those which are found in the great cemetery at Hallstatt in Austria, dating from the end of the Bronze Age.

Besides the car from Ystad, another remarkable relic of bronze, which was also probably used for temple worship, is preserved in the National Museum. It is a great crown-like ornament, which was found in 1847 in a peat-bog at Balkåkra, near Lund in Skåne. It was probably an ornamental mounting which had surrounded a large sacrificial vessel of wood (*Ant. suéd*, Fig. 254).

Several other discoveries of religious vessels have been made in other places in the North. For instance a large and beautiful bronze vase was found in 1862 in a peat-bog at Rönninge, in the island of Fyen; inside were eleven gold vessels with long handles. They belong to the later part of the Bronze Age, and were undoubtedly used in some temple, because they appear to be too precious to have been employed for private or secular purposes. In Sweden also a few similar gold

Fig. 92.—Gold vessel. Blek. ¼.

vessels have been found, but without handles (Fig. 92); and in 1886 a large bronze vase was also dug up in a peat-bog at Hedeskoga, in South Skåne (Fig. 93), in form, size, and ornamentation exactly like that found at Rönninge.

It is possible that the beautiful hanging vessels of bronze, which are found in very great numbers (Fig. 95), were used as lamps in temples or private dwellings.

82   ANCIENT SWEDISH CIVILISATION.   [CHAP.

Dome-shaped covers belonging to vessels of this kind are often found with them (Fig. 94).

The Danish antiquarian Worsaae has called attention to the many interesting finds of the Bronze Age made in the peat-bogs. He considers that their explanation

FIG. 93.

should be sought in some religious use, and he believes that they, as well as those great finds of the Earlier Iron Age, made also in the Danish peat-bogs, were originally offerings to the gods.

We have already seen that the dead were buried unburnt during the earlier part of the Bronze Age, but that they were burnt during the later part of that period (see p. 47).

FIG. 94.—Cover to bronze-vessel (Fig. 95).

FIG. 95.—Bronze hanging-vessel. V.-Götl. ½.

The unburnt bodies were usually laid in cists composed of flat stones placed edgewise, and covered with similar stones. In some parts of the North, especially in Jutland, coffins have been found made out of cloven and hollowed oak-trunks (see pp. 59, 60).

Those stone cists which contain several skeletons, and are often very large, appear to be the oldest; others are smaller, many only about six feet long, and contain a single extended skeleton. Some of these stone cists (as that at Hvidegård, for example, described below) even though of a full man's length, contain, strangely enough, no traces of an unburnt body, but only burnt bones. These probably belong to the beginning of the time when bodies were burnt. The remains of the burnt bodies when collected from the pyre were still often deposited in stone-cists. But these gradually became smaller and smaller, till at last we find them only about a foot long; there was no reason why they should be larger. Not unfrequently the burnt bones do not lie immediately in these small stone-cists, but in an earthenware vessel, which in that case is closely surrounded by the stones of the cist. Again the burnt bones often lie in earthenware vessels, without any such cist. Lastly, we sometimes find graves of the Bronze Age made up entirely of collections of burnt bones lying buried in the ground, and only covered by a flat stone (see Fig. 96). It is probable that these different kinds of graves actually followed each other in the order in which we have described them. Thus they form a gradual transition from the great grave chambers, and the stone cists with their many skeletons, of the Stone Age on the one side, to the insignificant graves with burnt bones at the end of the Bronze Age on the other.

THE BRONZE AGE.

The graves of the Bronze Age were usually covered with a barrow, which was made either chiefly of sand and earth, or of nothing but loose stones.[1] The same barrow very often contained several graves. The barrows are generally situated upon some height which commands an unimpeded view over the sea or some large lake. The cairns especially were often built up

FIG. 96.[2]—Section of a barrow at Dömmestorp in South Halland.

on a high hill, sometimes at a long distance from the present village.

Often, but not always, weapons, ornaments, &c., are found by the remains of the dead in graves of this period. In graves which contain unburnt bodies, we

---

[1] The barrows formed of stones are called cairns (*stenrösen* or *stenkummel*). Some of them do not however belong to the Bronze Age, but to other periods of heathen times. Often it is impossible to decide, without knowing their contents, to what period they belong.

[2] In the middle of the bottom of the barrow was a stone cist nearly seven feet long (*a*), containing an unburnt body and a bronze pin. Higher up were found three small stone cists containing burnt bones and antiquities of bronze. Close by the little cist at the top of the barrow stood a vessel filled with burnt bones, and near the cist marked *b* lay a heap of burnt bones, covered only by a flat stone.

not unfrequently find, just as in those of the Stone and Iron Ages, vessels of earthenware, and sometimes of wood,[1] which possibly once contained food. The graves of the later part of the Bronze Age do not appear to contain so many and so costly articles of bronze as those of the earlier part; it has been noticed particularly that weapons are comparatively seldom found in them.

The earthenware vessels, in which the burnt bones were laid, had frequently a bowl-shaped cover (Fig. 97). Most of them were undoubtedly used chiefly as burial-urns, which explains their simple form and lack of ornament. It seems to have been customary to make burial-urns coarse and plain.

FIG. 97.—Burial-urn with handle. Hall, ⅓.

One of the most remarkable discoveries in the graves of the Bronze Age yet known in the North was made in 1845, in a barrow at Hvidegård, not far from Copenhagen. In a stone cist of a full man's length, there was lying upon an animal's hide a heap of human bones, wrapped in a woollen mantle. By the side of

---

[1] A few wooden bowls made with a turning-lathe were found in Danish graves; they are ornamented with small and delicate pins made of tin. Two wooden boxes were discovered in the oak tree-coffin in Treenhöi described above on p. 59.

these lay a bronze sword in its sheath, a little bronze brooch, and also a leathern case containing the following somewhat miscellaneous collection : a piece of an amber bead, a small Mediterranean shell, a die made of deal, the tail end of a snake, a bird's claw, the lower jaw of a young squirrel, some very small stones, a small pair of tweezers, two bronze knives, and a spear-head of flint. This last had a piece of gut sewn round it in such a way that it could not be uncovered. The two bronze knives were also wrapped in leather. We can hardly be wrong in supposing that the dead man was either a doctor or a magician, or possibly both.

We have seen that during the Stone Age scarcely more than Götaland and some parts of Svealand were inhabited. The finds of the Bronze Age may be said to be confined within about the same limits. The southern provinces of the country, especially Skåne, continued to be much more thickly populated than the middle of Sweden. This is proved from the fact that, as far as we yet know, in every square mile on an average, at least twenty times as many bronze things of this period have been found in Skåne as in the rest of Sweden south of the river Dal-Elf.

The whole number of bronze antiquities from Sweden belonging to this period, as yet known, is about 4,000; of these only a little more than 200 were found in Svealand. From the whole of Norrland, which had no considerable population until the Iron Age, only very few antiquities of the Bronze Age are known, but two of them were found as far north as Medelpad. One is a remarkably well preserved bronze sword, found in Njurunda parish, the other a celt (Fig. 56) found in Timrå parish. In Finland, where antiquities of the Bronze Age are otherwise very scarce, a bronze sword was found in Storkyro parish, not far from Vasa, and therefore somewhat farther north than Medelpad. Even along the coast of Norway bronze weapons occur, though only occasionally, very far north, as far as North Trondhjem and Nordlands-Amts.

The Bronze Age in Sweden, as we have already seen, came to an end in the fifth century B.C.

Greece, as portrayed in the Homeric poems, was in the transition between the Bronze and the Iron Ages. Though iron is mentioned, bronze was still used for almost all purposes, even for weapons. It is probable that Homer's description of the heroic age of Greece would in more than one respect apply to the south of Scandinavia three thousand years ago, at least if we do not allow our eyes to be dazzled by the poetic shimmer which hangs around the heroes of the Trojan war. That the condition of Greece during its Bronze Age was actually in many ways like that of the North during the same stage of its civilisation, has also been proved by the remarkable finds lately made in Greece. It should however be borne in mind that the Bronze Age both began and ended in that country earlier than in the North.

On the other hand there are countries in which the Bronze Age ended much later than in Scandinavia. When the Europeans began their conquests in Mexico three hundred and seventy years ago, the Aztecs were living in a complete Bronze Age, without any knowledge of iron. And yet in many respects their civilisation was as high as that of which Europe could boast in the middle ages.

CHAPTER III.

THE IRON AGE.

(*From the Fifth Century* B.C. *to the latter half of the Eleventh Century* A.D.)

By "The Iron Age" is understood, as we have already seen, that part of *heathen times* in which iron was known. We might certainly say, if we regarded only the proper meaning of the words, that the Iron Age is even now still going on; but for the antiquarian's purposes the Iron Age in Sweden ends with the victory of Christianity over the Ása-gods.

During the Iron Age the inhabitants of Sweden became first acquainted with iron, silver, brass, lead, glass, stamped coins (of foreign production), and learnt the art of soldering and gilding metal, &c., &c. And as works of iron could not, like those of bronze, be produced only by casting, the smith's craft came to have far greater significance than it had had during the Bronze Age. But of the new discoveries of this period one of the most important was the art of writing, which the inhabitants of the North seem to have acquired soon after the beginning of the Christian era. The earliest alphabetical symbols in Sweden—indeed the only ones used in that country during the whole of heathen times —were the *runes*.

The large number of foreign coins which occur in finds of the Iron Age in the North, and a thorough study of the graves and antiquities of the same Age, have made it possible to distinguish what belong to the different parts of so long a period. At present we must however confine our attention to the four great main divisions:

A. The first part of the Earlier Iron Age, which includes the time from the fifth century B.C. to about the beginning of the Christian era.
B. The second part of the Earlier Iron Age, from about the beginning of the Christian era to the beginning of the fifth century A.D.
C. The first part of the Later Iron Age, from the beginning of the fifth to the beginning of the eighth century A.D.
D. The second part of the Later Iron Age, from the beginning of the eighth to the latter half of the eleventh century.

In every one of these divisions we can distinguish at least what belongs to the former and what to the latter half of the period.

A.—The First Part of the Earlier Iron Age.

(From the Fifth Century B.C. *to about the beginning of the Christian Era.)*

It was long supposed that the Iron Age in the North did not begin before the Christian era. The latest investigations have however shown that iron was known there much earlier. This we can hardly wonder at, considering that the new metal had, since before 500 years B.C., been in use among the Celtic peoples in Central Europe, with whom the Teutonic inhabitants of North Germany and Scandinavia had long had intercourse.

In Celtic countries the transition between the Bronze and the Iron Ages, including the earliest part of the Iron Age, is usually called the "Hallstatt Period," while a later part of the Earlier Iron Age in these countries is usually called the "Tène Period."

Many circumstances show that the first introduction of iron in the North coincides with the latter part of the Hallstatt period. Among other relics of the first part of the Swedish Iron Age we have collars, like those in Figs. 99 and 100, and round brooches like that in Fig. 98. The last are copies of a kind of brooch which is often found in Celtic graves of the Hallstatt period. The material of which they are made is certainly of the nature of bronze, but of a different mixture from that usual during the Bronze Age; it contains both lead and zinc [and is therefore properly speaking brass]. That

Fig. 98 *a, b*.—Bronze brooch with an iron pin. Öl. ½.

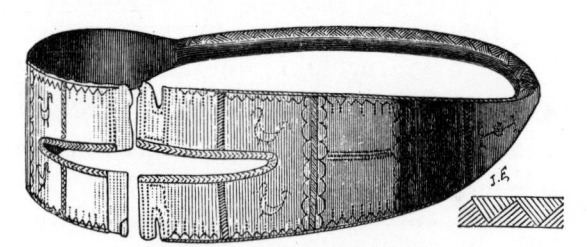

Fig. 99.—Bronze collar. Gotl. ½.

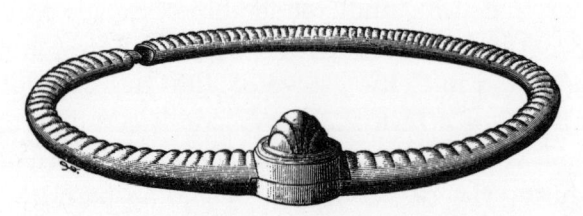

Fig. 100.—Bronze collar with a joint. Gotl. ½.

III.] THE IRON AGE. 93

FIG. 101.—Iron sword in a sheath of the same metal

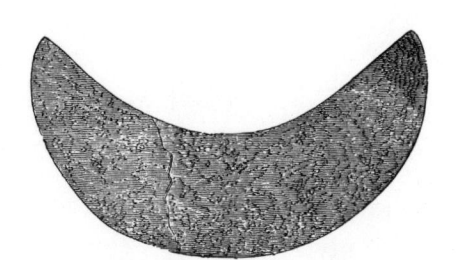

FIG. 102.—Iron knife. V.-Götl. ⅔.

FIG. 103.—Iron *fibula*. Boh. ½.

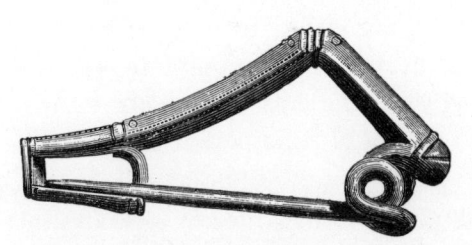

FIG. 104.—Bronze *fibula*. ¼.

they do not belong to the Bronze Age, but to a time when iron was in use, is further proved from the fact that the pins are always of iron.

Every year we are able to recognize more and more Northern antiquities which have forms peculiar to the Tène period or contemporary with it. Among objects characteristic of this time are swords with both blades and sheaths made of iron, like Fig. 101; thin crescent-shaped knives, like Fig. 102; *fibulæ*, often made of

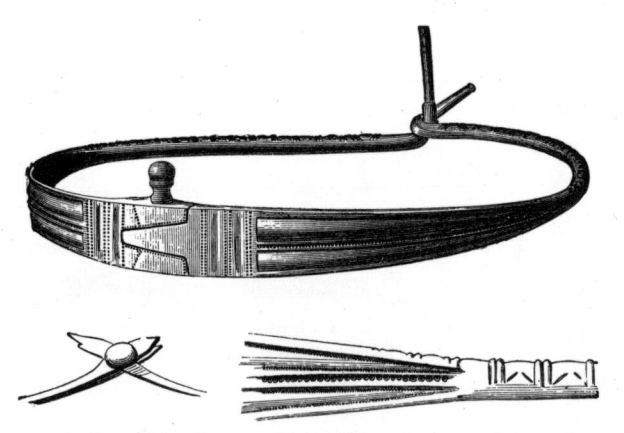

FIG. 105.—Bronze collar, with a joint. ½ and ¼.

iron, like Figs. 103, 104; collars, like 105, 107; and decorative plates of iron overlaid with bronze, like Fig. 106.

Many of these were found in graves containing burnt bones lying either in an earthenware urn, or laid in a little heap in the ground together with black mould. Graves of the latter kind are known as *brandpletter*.[1] The graves of this period are thus like those of the end

[1] On the island of Bornholm the Amtman Vedel discovered about 2,500 *brandpletter* and thereby made a valuable contribution to our knowledge of the earliest part of the Iron Age in the North.

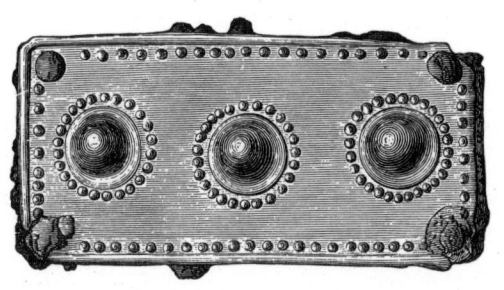

Fig. 106.—Iron plate for belt (?) overlaid with bronze. Ö.-Götl. ¼.

Fig. 107.—Bronze collar. V.-Götl ½.

of the Bronze Age, which also contain burnt bones either laid in an earthenware urn or put together in a heap.

This resemblance between the graves of the end of the Bronze Age and the beginning of the Iron Age, in conjunction with other circumstances, makes it more than probable that the first introduction of iron in the North was not connected with any immigration of a new people.

B.—The Second Part of the Earlier Iron Age.

(From about the beginning of the Christian Era to the beginning of the Fifth Century A.D.*)*

The antiquities of this period, even those which we must believe to be of native workmanship, are generally remarkable for their chaste and delicate ornaments. The cause of this must be sought undoubtedly in the great influence which Roman culture exercised in the North at this time. It is true that Roman armies never reached as far as Sweden, because the defeat of Varus in the Teutoburg Forest put an end for ever to the attempts of the Roman emperors to subdue the mighty Teutonic races. But by the peaceful ways of commerce the influence of Rome penetrated even to the people of the North. Great numbers of Roman coins have been found buried in Sweden, and also vessels of bronze and glass, weapons, &c., as well as works of art, all turned out of Roman workshops. These show that the ancestors of the Swedes had, during the first centuries of the Christian era, constant, even though not direct, communication with the foremost nation of their time.

But when we speak of "Roman workshops," we must not be supposed to mean that they were necessarily in Rome itself. Most of the Roman works found in the North, except the coins, certainly originated from the provinces of the empire. The Roman provinces which lay nearest to Scandinavia during the first centuries of our era were what is now England, the Netherlands, the part of Germany west of the Rhine, and that which is south of the Danube, as well as large districts of Austria and Hungary.

With very few exceptions[1] the oldest coins found in Sweden at present known are Roman, and by far the most of these are the silver coins known as *denarii*, which are rather larger than an English fourpenny piece, and were struck during the two first centuries of our era. In Fig. 108 we see a coin of this sort stamped with the head of Antoninus Pius, struck shortly after the emperor's death, which happened in 161 A.D.[2] It was found in the spring of the year 1871, together with a large number of other Roman silver coins struck between 54 and 211 A.D. They were found near the surface of the ground, in ploughing up a newly cultivated field at Hagestadborg in the parish of Löderup, in the south-east of Skåne. Five hundred and fifty of the coins, weighing together 3lbs., 9oz., were bought for the National Historical Museum. This is the largest hoard of the kind known in the whole of Scandinavia, if we except Gotland. Upon this island in 1842 at Kams, in Lummelunda parish, about 600 Roman silver coins were found

FIG. 108.—Roman silver coin (*denarius*). Sk. ¼.

---

[1] On the island of Gotland two Macedonian coins (of King Philip II.) and one Greek coin appear to have been found. The last was struck in the Grecian colony of Panormos (now Palermo) in Sicily.

[2] On the reverse side the pyre is figured, on which the emperor's body was burned.

belonging to the same period (the first and second centuries A.D.); and, while cleaning out a ditch in a field at Sindarfve, in Hemse parish, in 1870, some men came across about 1,500 silver coins of this kind preserved in an earthen crock. All these coins, as indeed most of the other Roman silver coins found in the North, were much worn; they weighed altogether about 9½lbs.

We must specially notice the fact that the hoard at Hagestadborg was found on the furthest south-easterly point of Skåne, the part of the mainland of Sweden lying nearest to Bornholm and the north of Germany; here too Roman coins have been often found before. This fact is particularly important, because the south-east of Skåne, Bornholm, Öland and Gotland are the parts of the North where incomparably the most Roman coins of the first two centuries A.D. have been found.[1]

To this we must add that large hoards of the same coins have been found at the mouth of the Vistula, and along the lower part of its course in Prussia, in Silesia near the Oder, and in Galicia. All this makes it more than probable that at least the greater number of the Roman coins of this time which came to the North were brought thither by commerce from the south-east along the valleys of the Vistula and the Oder.

Probably the same is true also of many of the other Roman works found in Scandinavia. Some of the coins and other objects however undoubtedly came from the south-west, from the Roman provinces on the Rhine.

[1] Out of about 4,760 Roman coins of this time at present known from Sweden, no less than 4,000 were found in the island of Gotland, 90 in Öland, 650 in Skåne, but only 23 on the mainland of Sweden, excluding Skåne. Besides these about 250 were found in Bornholm, and 600 in other parts of Denmark, but only 3 in Norway.

On the other hand the intercourse between Sweden and England during this period cannot have been very active.

Upon some of the Roman works found in Swedish and Danish soil we can still see the trade-mark, with the name of the factory or maker described usually in full. A bronze scoop with a trade-mark of this sort was found

FIG. 109.—Bronze vessel dedicated to Apollo Grannus, of Roman workmanship. Vestmanl. ⅕.

in 1828, together with an iron axe, in a barrow at Kungsgården, in the parish of Hög in north Helsingland;[1] and quite lately an iron sword was found in

[1] In Jutland a bronze scoop was found with the Roman name of the maker; the same name occurs again on four other scoops found, one in Hanover, two in England, and the fourth in Switzerland.

Öster-Götland with the letters MARCIM inscribed upon the blade (Fig. 113).

One of the most remarkable finds of Roman works hitherto known in Sweden, was made in the year 1818 at Fycklinge in Björksta parish, in the south-east of Vestmanland. Here was found in a barrow a large bronze vase filled with burnt bones (Fig. 109), and on it the following inscription:—APOLLINI. GRANNO. DONVM. AMMILLIVS. CONSTANS. PRÆF. TEMPLI. IPSIVS. V S L L M.,[1] which means that the vase was dedicated to Apollo Grannus by Ammillius Constans, the warden of his temple. How and when was this precious vessel brought from the Roman temple, to be used as a cinerary urn in a Swedish barrow, far away in a distant village of Vestmanland?

FIG. 110.—Part of an iron coat of mail. Sk. ¼.

Roman bronze vessels without inscriptions are frequently met with in Sweden, from Skåne as far as Medelpad, as well as in the islands of Öland and Gotland. Many of them were found in graves.

An unusually large and valuable find of Roman antiquities was made in 1872 near Abekås, a fishing village on the south coast of Skåne, west of Ystad. Here they found in a grave with the remains of a burnt body a large bronze vessel with two movable handles, a scoop with a bronze strainer belonging to it, two glass beakers (Fig. 112) and also pieces of an earthen vessel, of a coat of mail (Fig. 110), of iron weapons, of fine wool, &c., &c. (see *Ant. suéd.*, Figs. 373, 376, and 384).

[1] Apollini . . . Præfectus templi ipsius votum solvit libentissimo merito.

The bronze and glass vessels at any rate, and probably the coat of mail, are Roman work.

In 1837 some people who were engaged in harvesting at Ösby, in the parish of Gräsgård in Öland, found a bronze statuette of Juno 11in. high (Guide, Fig. 113). This beautiful figure probably dates from the latter part of the second century A.D. In the same island a leg belonging to another bronze statuette has also been found, besides a bull of massive bronze. The latter, which weighs about 9lbs., 13oz., they found in 1845 while ploughing a field at Lilla Frö in Resmo parish; in its middle there is a large quadrangular hole (see *Ant. suéd.*, Fig. 370). We also know of one Roman bronze statuette from Upland (Fig. 111); it was found in the Fysing Lake.

Besides the two just mentioned from Abekås, Roman glass beakers belonging to the time in question, have been found in many other places in Sweden, in Skåne, Bohuslän, Vester-Götland, Upland, Medelpad, Öland, and Gotland.

FIG. 111.—Roman bronze statuette. Upl. ⅓.

We ought also to regard as Roman works a large number at any rate of the many glass beads of the Iron Age found in Swedish graves. Several of them have remarkably beautiful figures of many colours. Roman works decorated with enamel have also been sometimes found in Sweden (see Guide, Fig. 81).

THE IRON AGE.

In other parts of Scandinavia also, and especially in Denmark, a large number of Roman works of the first few centuries have been found; such as, for example, vessels of bronze, silver, glass, and earthenware, bronze statuettes, a small bronze mirror, glass beads, and iron weapons. Of the latter we may specially mention a bronze helmet, the boss of a shield with the owner's

FIG. 112.—Glass beaker, of Roman workmanship. Ol. ½

name in Roman letters, iron sword blades with Roman trade-marks, coats of mail, &c.

But besides all these objects of Roman workmanship the finds of the earlier Iron Age contain many different objects which were obviously made in the North, though they often show clearly the influence of Roman models. We may regard as native works of this time, for instance, a large number of weapons, gold rings, bracelets (Fig. 114), buckles, and other ornaments, earthen vessels, and some well-built boats found in a Danish peat bog, &c., &c.

The finds of this age contain also a large number of tools and implements, such as anvils, tongs, sledges, hammers, axes, punches, gimlets, awls, scissors, knives, scrapers, planes, and files —all of iron; and also rivets, nails, one crucible, &c.

The weapons are mainly of the same kinds as under the Bronze Age, but of different forms. The swords are designed for cutting and not only for thrusting; they are therefore provided with a crossguard, which is however short. The blades, always of iron, have sometimes one, sometimes two edges. They are not unfrequently chased, and often made in a way which betokens a high degree of skill. The greater part of the hilt is almost always made of wood or horn; sometimes overlaid with bronze or silver; occasionally it is entirely of bronze.

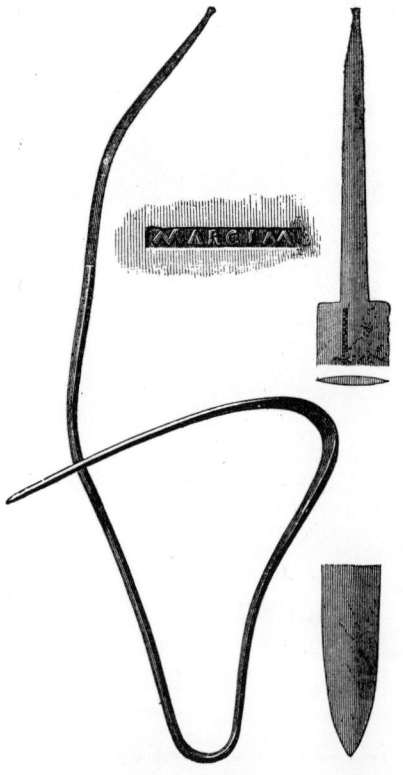

Fig. 113.—Iron sword with maker's mark. Ö.-Götl. ¼ and ¼.

Remains of sword sheaths are often found; some few have been preserved whole. They are made of wood with chapes of metal or ivory. The leather belts from which the swords were hung have also been found in Danish peat-bogs. On one of them a dolphin and other figures had been very tastefully embroidered, as shown by

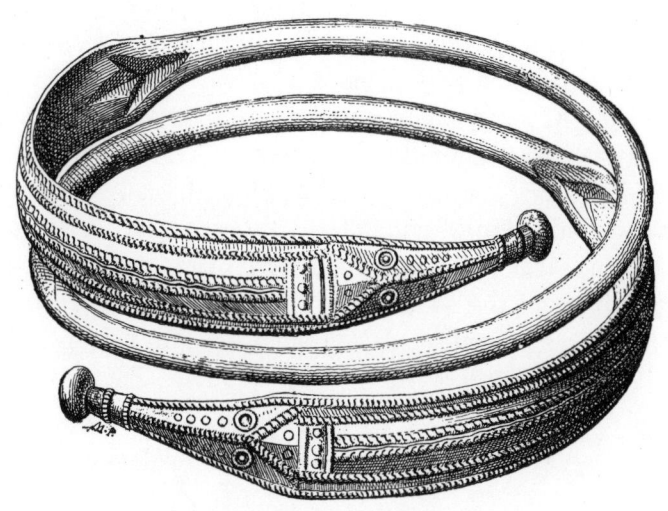

FIG. 114. Spiral gold bracelet. Ol. ¼.

the holes of the stitches still clearly visible. This too betokens a Roman influence.

The spear or lance appears to have been a still commoner weapon than the sword. Both the iron heads and the wooden shafts, which were sometimes as much as eleven feet long, are found preserved. In those used as missiles the centre of gravity was often marked by driving in a tack or tying round a piece of string, in order that the thrower might quickly and easily poise the spear in his hand.

We find not only the heads of arrows, usually of

iron, but also several shafts and bows. The latter are made of wood about six feet long, and are exactly like the bows still used by several non-European peoples. Bows with a stock, like the cross-bows of the Middle Ages, were unknown in Sweden in heathen times. The arrows had wooden shafts from two to three feet long; at their butt end we see traces of four rows of feathers which were bound with pitched thread. The mark of the owner was often cut on the shaft in order that he might easily recognize his weapon again; some of these marks are evidently runes.

Besides these a quiver was once found made entirely of wood, and large enough to hold some score of arrows, and also a few mountings of brass belonging to other quivers of the same kind.

Fig. 115 represents a horn belonging to this period found in a peat-bog in Södermanland. The middle portion of it is made of an ox-horn, of which only part remains; broad mountings of bronze are fixed to both ends.

The shields were round and flat, and were made by joining together several thin planed pieces of wood. The diameter varies from two to about four feet. Round the edge there is sometimes a fine rim of bronze, or occasionally of silver. In the middle there is a hole for the handle; the hand was protected by a boss of iron, bronze, silver, or wood, fastened over the hole (see Guide, Fig. 116, and *Ant. suéd.*, 289, 290).

Besides shields we now find also other defensive weapons, namely, the coats of mail already mentioned, which were probably of Roman origin, and helmets. A Roman bronze helmet was discovered in a peat-bog at Thorsbjerg in South Jutland. And in the same bog was

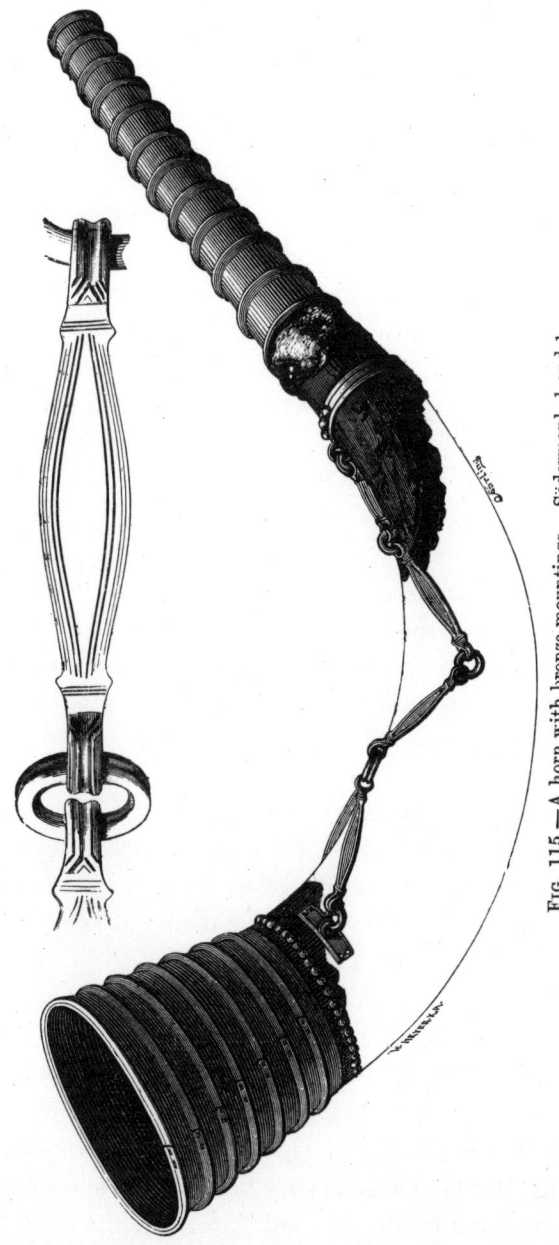

FIG. 115.—A horn with bronze mountings. Södermanl. ¼ and ¼.

also found a beautiful helmet of silver, overlaid with gold. It was evidently of "barbarian," that is to say not Roman, workmanship. It is to be seen on Fig. 116.

It is mainly through the unexpected and lucky discoveries in some Danish peat-bogs that we have got to know the state of civilisation in the North during the earlier Iron Age. Through the wonderful power which peat possesses of preserving even the most delicate and, under ordinary circumstances, most perishable materials, we have here an opportunity of getting to know such things as their clothes and their wooden implements, &c. It is by the help of these finds, and especially those in the peat-bogs of Thorsbjerg and Nydam in South Jutland, that we have been able to give such a picture of a Northern warrior of about 300 A.D. as we see in Fig. 116. Every line of this picture is true to history, because both clothes, weapons, and ornaments are exactly copied from what has been actually found in these two bogs.

The clothes are made of wool; the weaving, which is finer than was usual during the Bronze Age, seems to be a sort of diaper-work, often in a check pattern. The most important garments are a long jacket, with sleeves reaching to the wrists, and breeches which are fastened round the waist with a strap (not shown in the drawing), and sewn on to a pair of socks below. The outer clothing of the feet consists of a kind of leather sandals, decorated with fine tooled ornaments. A woollen mantle with a long fringe below is thrown over the shoulders. One of the mantles found in the bog at Thorsbjerg had preserved its colour; it was green, with yellow and dark-green borders.

FIG. 116.—Northern warrior of about 300 A.D.

110 ANCIENT SWEDISH CIVILISATION. [CHAP.

We also see on Fig. 116 almost all the weapons lately described: a helmet of silver-gilt; a coat of mail composed of iron rings, and decorated on the breast with two beautiful round plates of bronze and silver-gilt; a wooden shield with a boss and rim of metal; a sword, bow and arrows, and the quiver hanging on the back.

The clothes were usually fastened together during the Iron Age with pins or *fibulæ*, and not, as now, with buttons or hooks. A beautiful *fibula* of a form common during this period is seen in Fig. 117. Fig. 118 represents a buckle belonging to a

FIG. 117.—*Fibula* of silver-gilt. Gotl. ¼.

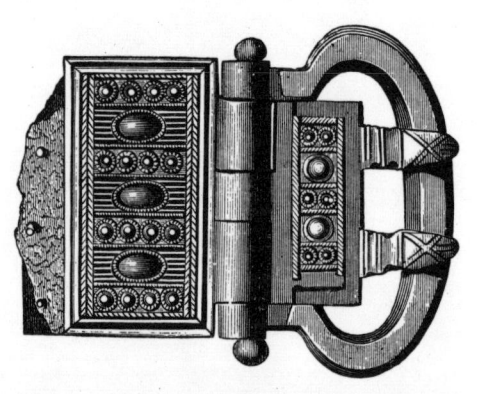

FIG. 118.—Bronze buckle, overlaid with silver gilt and set with coloured glass. Upl. ¼.

belt. The ornaments worn at this time were rings, pendants, &c., of gold (Figs. 114, 119, 120); beads of

III.]   THE IRON AGE.   111

gold, glass, amber, &c. On the other hand the bronze collars, so abundant during the last part of the Bronze Age, had by this time almost entirely disappeared. Gold collars are also very scarce. Silver, so universal during the later Iron Age, was still used very little.

Among articles of toilette we might also mention combs of bone, small silver boxes, probably used for

FIG. 119.—Gold ring.
Medelp. ¼.

FIG. 120.—Gold pendant.
Öl. ¼.

ointments, and small tweezers and ear-picks usually of bronze, but occasionally of silver. Such tweezers, sometimes joined to an ear-pick by a little ring, were probably used instead of razors to remove the beard.

We now meet with a novelty among sewing implements in the shape of scissors, which, as we have already seen, are never found in graves or hoards of the Bronze Age. The scissors of the Iron Age are, like our ordinary shears, always made of a single piece.

Of household goods we now meet for the first time with spoons and drinking horns; at any rate there are none known of the Bronze Age. The spoons were usually made of wood; but in a Danish grave a silver spoon was found, probably of Roman origin. The parts of the drinking horns best-preserved are, as we might have expected, the mouthpieces and tips of bronze, but sometimes traces of the horn itself are still found; it seems to have generally been an ordinary ox-horn. These, like

Fig. 121.—Silver cup partly gilded. Denmark ½.

other vessels, used often to follow the dead into the grave. Strangely enough we not unfrequently find remains of *two* horns in the same grave, though only *one* body seems to have been buried there. In Denmark and Norway some costly glass drinking vessels were found shaped like horns.

Besides horns, a number of other vessels of this period have been found, partly of Roman workmanship, made of glass, bronze, silver (Fig. 121) and especially wood (Fig. 122) and earthenware. The last, which must have been in almost all cases made in the country, are generally much finer, thinner, and better baked than those of the Bronze Age; the shape is often

FIG. 122.—Wooden bucket with bronze platings. Norway ½.

very graceful (Fig. 123). Like those of the two earlier periods, they are never glazed.

We often find by the drinking vessels in graves of both the earlier and later Iron Age, a sort of draughts and dice. The former are made of bone, glass, amber or earthenware; they are round, flat on the under side, but

114   ANCIENT SWEDISH CIVILISATION.   [CHAP.

convex above. The dice are either much like those used in the present day, or of a longer and narrower shape. The sides are marked with the numbers from 1 to 6. Large pieces of the boards marked with checks were once found in a Danish peat-bog among other relics of this period.

Native coins of this Age have not yet been discovered in any Northern land; the first in Sweden were struck by Olaf Skötkonung, at the end of the heathen times.

FIG. 123.—Earthenware ewer.   Gotl. $\frac{1}{3}$.

We have already spoken of the Roman coins of the first two centuries found in this country. For payment they sometimes used these coins, sometimes worked or unworked gold and silver by weight. Small bronze balances have been found in graves of the earlier Iron Age; these are probably of Roman origin, because they are exactly like those which the Romans used. They also resemble those in use at the present day, consisting of a balance with a scale hanging from either end.

THE IRON AGE.

The foreign coins as well as the many other objects from foreign countries found in the North show that the commerce and communication with other lands during the Earlier Iron Age must have been very considerable.

The usual method of travelling by land was riding on horseback; the wares were carried on pack-horses. Bridles (see *Ant. suéd*, Figs. 297-9), spurs (see Guide, Fig. 77), and other things of the sort belonging to this time, have been often found; but stirrups do not appear to have come into use till the Later Iron Age. We get representations of carts in Sweden, even of the Bronze Age, as we have already seen; and in some Danish finds of the Earlier Iron Age, some very well preserved carts have been actually found.

One of the most remarkable finds of the Earlier Iron Age was that made in 1863, in the peat-bog of Nydam in South Jutland, already mentioned. There were found two "clinch-built" boats, with Roman coins of the second century A.D., and a large number of other things from the Earlier Iron Age, of which most had obviously been placed in the boat. One of the boats was made of oak (Fig. 124), the other of pine. They were large and open, pointed at both ends, designed only for rowing, with no trace of a mast. Both boats differ from those now generally in use, by the peculiar way in which the planks are fastened to the ribs. The oak boat, which is remarkable for its very supple and graceful form, is 78 ft. between the high points at the stem and stern, and 10 ft. 9 in. broad midships; it was rowed with fourteen pairs of oars. These are exactly like those still used in the North, and are 11 ft. 2 in. long. The rudder is narrow, and was fastened to one side of the

116   ANCIENT SWEDISH CIVILISATION.   [CHAP.

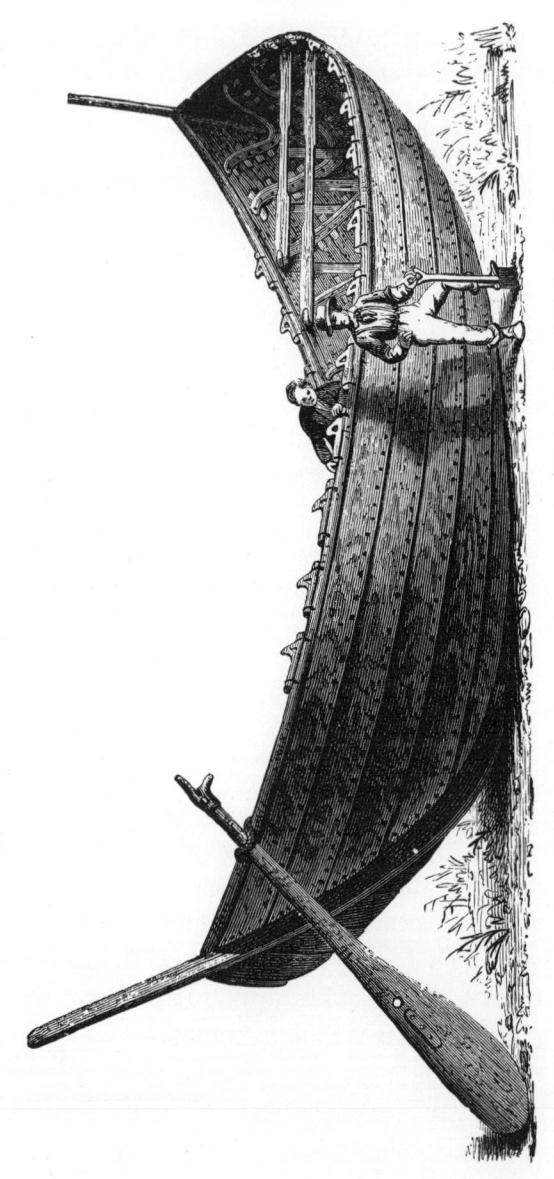

FIG. 124.—Boat for 14 pairs of oars, found at Nydam in South Jutland.

boat near the stern end. Other things found belonging to boats, were a large iron anchor, two scoops, &c.

During the later part of the heathen times the boats were always drawn up on land for the winter, or when they were not wanted for some time. The boats found at Nydam have holes at the ends, for the rope by which they were hauled on land.

In a peat-bog at Fiholm in Vestmanland, some remains of a boat were found not many years ago, which seems to have been built in the same way as those we have just described.

The runes used during the earlier and middle parts of the Iron Age are generally known as the Earlier Runes, and are very distinct from the Later Runes found upon the runic stones, which are so common, especially in the district of the Mälar Lake. Upon a gold "bracteate" (Fig. 131) found near Vadstena, and belonging to the fifth century A.D., we find the whole set[1] of the Earlier Runes arranged in the following way :—

ᚠ ᚢ ᚦ ᚨ ᚱ ᚲ ᚷ ᚹ : ᚺ ᚾ ᛁ ᛃ ᛇ ᛈ ᛉ ᛊ : ᛏ ᛒ ᛖ ᛗ ᛚ ᛜ ᛟ [2]
f u th a r k g w : h n i j (a) ? p -r s : t b e m l ng o

---

[1] The expression "Runic alphabet" is usually avoided, because the runes are not, like the Greek, Latin, and modern alphabets, arranged so as to begin with A, B, corresponding, of course, to the Greek "alpha" and "beta," from which the word "alphabet" is derived.

[2] The runes ᚦ and ᚹ probably represented the same sound as the English *th* in "that" and the English *w*. The rune ᛉ is at this period used as a final letter; its original sound was *s*, but by a change in the language itself it afterwards became *r*.

Besides the runes stamped on this ornament some others also occur during the period in question, as for example ᛗ $= d$.

A glance at these symbols is enough to show their close relationship to the Latin letters, at any rate in their earliest forms. ᚦ ᚱ ᚲ ᚺ ᛁ ᛋ ᛏ ᛒ ᛉ are found almost unchanged in the Latin D R C H I S T B O, which represent the same sounds as the corresponding runes, the Latin C being pronounced hard like K. Many of the other runes also, if closely examined, will be seen to be not unlike the equivalent Latin letters; for example the runes ᚢ and ᛚ are the inverted Latin U and L, and so forth. By a careful comparison we find too that the runes show a nearer relationship to the Latin alphabet than to any other. In most cases, where the runes differ from the Latin letters, the difference can be explained from the fact that the former seem to have been originally designed for carving on wood. This made it necessary to avoid all horizontal strokes, because being with the grain of the wood, they would easily become obliterated. Also curved lines could only be produced on wood with difficulty. The earliest runes therefore consist only of perpendicular and slanting strokes.

The latest investigations have proved that the runes arose from an alteration of the Latin letters. Probably they were invented a little before the Christian era by a South Teutonic tribe, in imitation of the Roman writing, which the Teutons received from one of the Keltic tribes living just to the north of the Alps.

The earliest known runic inscriptions of which we can determine the date are those found upon some weapons and tools belonging to those great finds in the Danish bogs already described. Their date is about 300 A.D. We also know of many Swedish inscriptions with the earlier runes belonging to this time and the following centuries.

They are found on fourteen stones,[1] on a buckle of silver-gilt from Ethelhem in Gotland (Figs. 136, 137), on an amulet (?) of bone from a bog at Lindholm in Skåne, on the remarkable gold bracteate from Vadstena just described, and also upon twenty-six other gold bracteates from Skåne, Bleking, Halland, Vester-Götland, and the island of Gotland. A runic stone from Tanum in North Bohuslän is given in Fig. 125. The inscription runs as follows:—THRAWINGAN HAITINAR WAS,—which means, " (The stone) was called Thrawinge's."

Inscriptions with the early runes are also found in Norway on stones, gold bracteates, &c., and in Denmark, upon the boss of a shield, the chape of a sword-sheath, on some arrows, a plane, a gold horn, a gold ring, a comb, as well as on some *fibulæ* and gold bracteates. They occur also in England in great numbers, in France (Burgundy), in Germany, in Wallachia (upon a large massive gold ring), and the west of Russia. All belong to about the same date, and are of Teutonic origin.

The fact that runic inscriptions are found not only on the memorial stones raised over departed relatives, but also on many things connected with daily life, such as

[1] Five of these stones with early runes are in Bleking (viz. at Björketorp, Gommor, Istaby, Stentoften, and Sölvesborg), two in Bohuslän (at Tanum and Räfsal), one in Vermland (at Varnum, near Kristinehamn), one in Vester-Götland (at Vånga), one Öster-Götland in the churchyard at Rök, two in Södermanland (at Berga and Skääng,) and two in Upland (at Möjebro in Hagby parish and Krogstad).

ornaments, weapons, and tools, seems to show that the knowledge of runes was not restricted to a few, but was generally spread among the people.

Although these early runic inscriptions do not contain

FIG. 125.—Runic Stone at Tanum in Bohuslän.

any accounts of historically-known persons or events, they are yet of the very greatest historical importance. By them we learn many interesting facts bearing upon the civilisation of the people; and above all we get to know something of their language. They are the earliest written records in Sweden, eight or nine centuries before the first documents on vellum still surviving.[1] They show that during the Earlier Iron Age the speech, and therefore the people, were Teutonic; but they show also, and this is of great importance, that the language spoken in the fourth and fifth centuries A.D. was very much, though not quite, like that spoken by the Goths on the Danube during the same period.

To the end of the period now under discussion belong the two beautiful gold horns which were found—the one in 1639, the other in 1734—in nearly the same place at Gallehus in Jutland, but were stolen away in 1802 from the *Kunstkammar* in Copenhagen and melted down. They together weighed 13 lbs. Round the mouth of one of them there was a long runic inscription. It is supposed, doubtless with very good reason, that these horns were used as trumpets in a temple, and that the figures represented on them have a mythological meaning. The runic inscription does not help us here, because it gives only the maker's name.

We have no other direct information, certainly, concerning the religion of the Swedes during this part of the Iron Age, but we may reasonably suppose that it much resembled the religion of the Later Iron Age, as we know it from the Eddas. Thor was probably the chief god, and the number of place-names still surviving which testify to his worship—such as Thorsharg (now Thorshälla), Thorslunda, Thorsvi, and others—no doubt

[1] The earliest Swedish MS. on vellum dates from 1160–70, the first known example of paper so used in Sweden dates from about 1340.

generally point to the places where the people during the earliest part of the Iron Age, if not before, offered to the god of thunder and of war. The great Danish hoards so often mentioned before seem also to have been originally offerings made by a victorious army to the god who gave them victory. In connexion with this we should remember that it was in a bog in *Thorsbjerg* that one of the most valuable of these hoards was discovered.

In the majority of Swedish graves of the Earlier Iron Age we find burnt bones, in others remains of unburnt bodies. The burnt bones were usually preserved in a vessel of earthenware or bronze (see p. 101). The unburnt bodies were pretty frequently found lying, especially in the islands of Gotland and Öland, in stone cists, built of flat stones set up edgewise like those of the Bronze Age already described (see p. 84). When the dead were not burnt they seem to have been buried with their clothes and ornaments, the men with their weapons. We sometimes find on the breast of the dead the central boss and other remains of a shield, intended, it would seem, to protect the warrior even in death. By the side of the body, as we have already seen, we often find drinking-horns, glass beakers, or other vessels, besides draughts, dice, &c. Even in graves with burnt bones we generally find ornaments, weapons, &c., often injured by fire, which in most cases shows, no doubt, that they had followed the dead on to the pyre.

The graves of the Earlier Iron Age in Sweden were usually covered by a barrow or a cairn (Fig. 126). Sometimes we find however, in Skåne for example, graves (with unburnt bodies) of this period which—

THE IRON AGE.

FIG. 126.—Cemetery near Greby in Bohuslän.

like the *brandpletter* of the first part of the Iron Age, and the graves in Christian churchyards—lie under the natural surface of the ground. There is not, now at least, any trace of them on the ground above. It is common to find graves of this kind crowded together. Many cemeteries of this sort are known in Denmark.

C.—The First Part of the Later Iron Age.

(From the beginning of the Fifth to the beginning of the Eighth Century A.D.)

When Italy had been overrun by the "barbarians," the old civilisation found undisturbed shelter only in that part of the Roman empire which was subject to Byzantine rule. It is very interesting therefore to find so many traces of an active intercourse with Byzantium in the relics dug up yearly out of Swedish soil.

The relics which have most to tell us are the Byzantine gold coins of the fifth century, which, together with the contemporary gold coins of the western half of the Roman empire, have been found very plentifully in Scandinavia, especially in Sweden.[1] In Fig. 127 we have a coin struck during the reign of the Emperor Libius Severus.

Fig. 127.—Roman gold coin (solidus). Öl. ¼.

We shall find that this stream of gold flowing from Byzantium was much larger still, if we bear in mind that most of the beautiful gold ornaments in which the

[1] More than 260 coins of this period coming from the eastern and western divisions of the Roman empire have been found in Sweden alone. The majority of them (more than 200) were found in the islands of Öland and Gotland. In Öland alone were found more than a third of all that are yet known in the North.

126   ANCIENT SWEDISH CIVILISATION.   [CHAP.

Swedish finds of this period are so rich seem to have been made in that country out of Roman and Byzantine coins melted down.

The source of this stream is to be found in the

Fig. 128.—Gold collar. Södermanl. ⅔.

tribute of gold, which history tells us that many of the Byzantine emperors had to pay to the Goths on the Danube. They are the very same emperors whose

III.] THE IRON AGE. 127

names appear on the coins found in Sweden. By the help of the hoards of coins we can also easily trace the lines along which this gold tribute found its way to the relatives of the Goths upon the coasts of the Baltic. These lines were along the valleys of the great rivers, especially the Vistula,[1] through what are now Poland and the east of Germany.

A glance at the beautiful golden ornaments of this period preserved in the National Museum is enough to show how rich in gold Sweden must then have been. Gold rings of about 2lbs. weight or more have often been found in that country. The largest hoard of gold yet found in Sweden, and one of the largest ever found in the whole of Europe, was that discovered in 1774 at Thureholm in Södermanland, near Trosa. The hoard altogether weighed more than 27lbs. We have still preserved from it in the National Museum a large and beautiful collar of fine gold, weighing 2lbs. 3oz. (Fig. 128), and also handsome gold plates belonging to a sword-hilt, and two sword-sheaths (Fig. 129, see also *Ant. suéd.*, Figs. 408, 409, 418,

Fig. 129.—Gold plate of a sword-sheath. Södermanl. ¼.

---

[1] That the ordinary lines of commerce between South Europe and Scandinavia followed the course of the Vistula is also shown by the fact that the Gothic historian Jordanes (or Jornandes), bishop in Ravenna, describes "the island of Scanzia"—*i.e.* Skåne, or Sweden—as lying opposite the mouth of the Vistula.

FIG. 130.—Gold collar with joint. Öl. ¾.

419).[1] The most beautiful gold ornaments of this period yet found in the North are three large broad collars weighing from about 1lb. 6oz. to 1lb. 13oz.

They consist of several (three, five, or seven) hollow rings lying one upon the other, and decorated with fine filigree work and other ornaments soldered on. At the back there is a hinge, and in front the ends of the rings fit inside each other, and so the whole is made secure. Two of these collars were found in Vester-Götland and the third in Öland (Fig. 130). No other of the kind has, as far as we know, been found in any other country.

As there were yet no native coins in Sweden, gold by weight was used for payments. We often find buried in this country larger and smaller smooth gold rings of a spiral form, which were evidently used as a means of exchange. They are frequently broken off at one (Fig. 133), sometimes at both, ends.

The gold pendants, or "bracteates" as they are called—an ornament of this period much like a coin or medal—which are so often found in Sweden, were doubtless merely personal ornaments worn by all who had the wish and means to procure them [2] (Figs. 131, 132). There is no reason to suppose that they were like the medals now worn as rewards or as marking an order of merit. Sometimes several of these are found in the same spot together with beads of gold or glass.

[1] At Broholm in Fyen, in Denmark, a hoard of gold was found in 1832 consisting of rings, gold pendants, &c., weighing 7lbs. 10oz. See also the account of the horn found at Gallehus on p. 121.

[2] We must not confuse with these gold "bracteates" the small, thin silver coins of the middle ages, which are stamped only on one side; though these are frequently called by the same name. The name is derived from the Latin *bractea*, "a thin plate."

130 ANCIENT SWEDISH CIVILISATION. [CHAP.

They were probably all strung together and wound round the neck; the beads were put between the

FIG. 131.—Gold bracteate with a list of runes. Ö.-Götl. ¼.

FIG. 132.—Gold bracteate. Boh. ¾.

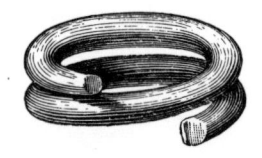

FIG. 133.—Gold finger-ring with one end broken off. Öl. ¼.

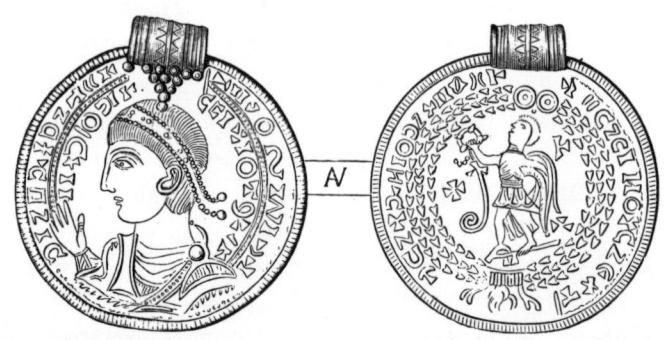

FIG. 134.—Gold bracteate, a "barbarian" copy of a Roman coin. Boh. ¼.

bracteates to prevent them from knocking against each other. Some grave-finds prove that such ornaments were worn both by men and women.

THE IRON AGE.

Many of these bracteates have upon them the figure of a human head above that of a four-footed animal (Fig. 131), and were originally copies of Roman coins of the fourth century (Fig. 134). It has been thought that some of them may possibly have been intended to represent Thor or some other god; the animal has sometimes a narrow pointed beard which gives it the appearance of a goat, an animal which we know to have been sacred to Thor.

Other pendants of this sort have interlacing ornaments terminating in animal forms (Fig. 132). This should be specially noticed, because it shows that the taste for this kind of decoration which was so beautifully developed during the last centuries of the Iron Age already existed at the time we are speaking of.

The bracteates not unfrequently bear runic inscriptions.[1] They were generally stamped. The figures in relief on the front usually correspond to depressions on the back, which is otherwise quite smooth. Round these raised figures there are often fine decorations made with a punch. The loop is sometimes ornamented with beautiful filigree work. The largest golden bracteate yet known is one recently found in Skåne (see Guide, Fig. 122), which is $4\frac{7}{8}$ inches in diameter.

These bracteates, often the result of great skill, must be regarded as native productions, because they are found very plentifully in the North;[2] whereas very few

[1] On the bracteate (given in Fig. 131) which was found at Vadstena we have a complete list of the old runes. See p. 177.

[2] More than 200 gold bracteates of the same kind as in Fig. 131, and more than 100 bracteates with animal interlacings, as in Fig. 132, have been found in Sweden, Norway, and Denmark.

132   ANCIENT SWEDISH CIVILISATION.   [CHAP.

ornaments of this kind occur in other lands, and then usually under circumstances which make it very probable that they came from Scandinavia.

The bow-shaped *fibulæ* so usual during the Earlier Iron Age (Fig. 117), had gradually developed into the large and handsome forms common during the period under discussion (Figs. 135, 136). These brooches are distinguished both by their peculiar shape and their somewhat "barbarous" ornamentation. We see no longer the Roman influence so visible in the preceding centuries. *Fibulæ* of the same sort, but with some slight variations, are also found in all countries inhabited by Teutonic races during the fifth and sixth centuries. They are usually of bronze or silver, often gilded, and sometimes inlaid with garnets or pieces of coloured glass.

FIG. 135.—*Fibula* of silver gilt.
Öl. ⅔.

Upon the back of a *fibula* (Figs. 136, 137) found at Ethelhem, in Gotland, we find the following inscription in runes—*Ek Er(i)la w(o)rta*, meaning "I Jarl made (it)."[1]

[1] The rune for E has here the form ᛖ instead of the usual form ᛗ.

THE IRON AGE.

Besides the gold coins from Byzantium, the gold spirals, gold bracteates, and many other objects of gold as well as the large *fibulæ*, we should also ascribe to

FIG. 136.—Buckle of silver gilt. Gotl. ¼.

this part of the Iron Age swords with hilts like those represented in Figs. 138 and 141. Such hilts were usually made of silver-gilt or gilded bronze. The triangular pommel is sometimes decorated with beautiful interlacing ornaments. Some of those found in Sweden are made of solid gold. One, found in Qville parish, Bohuslän, (Guide, Fig. 118) is decorated with inlaid

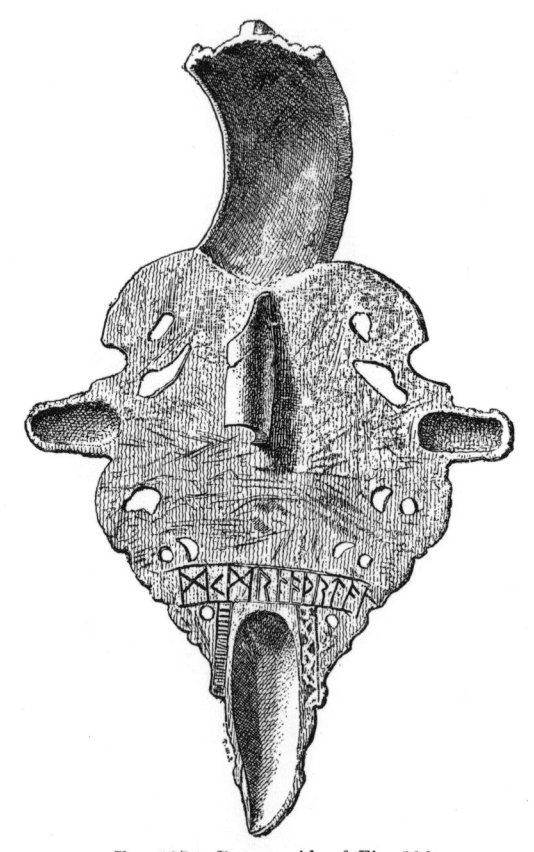

FIG. 137. Reverse side of Fig. 136.

garnets, like that represented in Fig. 138. A few pommels have also been found decorated with massive gold tops[1] as seen in the same figure. We have

[1] One, weighing nearly 8 oz., was found in 1862 at Qvicksta, near Strengnäs.

III.] THE IRON AGE. 135

already spoken of the gold mountings found at Thureholm (see p. 127). Many other similar pieces of pure gold, which also once belonged to the hilts and sheaths

Fig. 138. Upper part of an iron sword with hilt of gilded bronze. The triangular pommel is of gold inlaid with garnets. Gott. ⅔.

of swords, and are of the same date, have been found in other places in Sweden. Some of them have beautiful filigree ornaments (Guide, Fig. 119).

136   ANCIENT SWEDISH CIVILISATION.   [CHAP.

The ornamentation on many of the objects of this period found in the North (Figs. 139, 140) points to the influence of Irish art. It is therefore more than

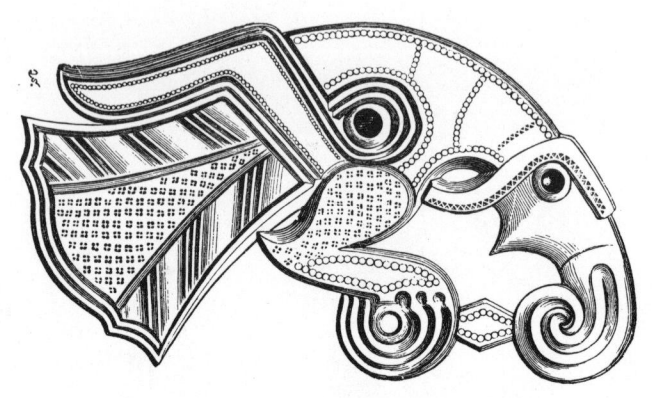

FIG. 139.—Ornament of gilded bronze. Gotl. ¼.

probable that the ancient Swedes, even before the beginning of the Viking Period proper, had direct communication, whether peaceful or warlike, with the British Isles. The poems of Ossian seem also to point

FIG. 140.—A plate of gilded bronze. Gotl. ¼.

to early relations between Scotland and the western side of the Scandinavian peninsula.

One of the most remarkable finds of this period is one made in 1855 in a barrow at Ultuna, near the river Fyris, south of Upsala. In this barrow were found

III.] THE IRON AGE. 137

Fig. 141.—Upper part of an iron sword with hilt of gilded bronze. Upl. ⅔

138   ANCIENT SWEDISH CIVILISATION.   [CHAP.

the mouldering, but yet visible, remains of a large boat in which a man had been buried with his weapons and horses.[1] The nails which had kept the timbers together were still in their places. By the side of the unburnt body lay a sword. The blade was made of iron, and the beautiful hilt of gilded bronze with very graceful interlacing ornaments, (Fig. 141). Traces were also found of the wooden sheath and its gilded chape. There were besides these an iron helmet with a

FIG. 142.—Boss of a shield made of iron with bronze plating. Upl. ½.

crest of silver-plated bronze, the boss of a shield with beautiful bronze plating (Fig. 142), a shield-handle, nineteen arrow-heads, the bits of two bridles, all of iron; and in addition to these thirty-six draughts[2] and three dice made of bone. There were also parts of two skeletons of horses. In the forepart of the boat were

[1] We shall have occasion to speak of similar finds made in Sweden and Norway, especially of two boats found in barrows in Norway which are wonderfully well preserved.

[2] One of the draughts was distinguished from the rest by a metal mounting, a circumstance noticed in other sets of draughts belonging to the Iron Age.

III.] THE IRON AGE. 139

a gridiron and a pot made of iron plates nailed together and having a movable handle, some bones of pigs and geese. These are relics either of the funeral feast, or of the food given to the dead.

Near the church at Vendel in North Upland several graves have lately been discovered, belonging partly to this, partly to the following, period. Most of them contained large boats about thirty feet long, in which the dead were buried with their weapons, horses, and other domestic animals. In one grave was found the skeleton of a falcon. Of these weapons we may specially mention a beautiful sword and a helmet (Figs. 143, 144; see also Guide, Figs. 128—131). In another grave lay an exquisite bridle of gilded and enamelled bronze (see Guide, Fig. 132). It rested upon the head of a horse that had been buried with the dead warrior. These graves, which all contained remains of unburnt bodies, were not covered with a barrow, but lay deep in the ground.

FIG. 143.—Chape of gilded bronze. Upl. ¼.

In other graves of the same period we find remains of burnt bodies.

To this time we must refer the three great barrows

near the church of Old Upsala, which are still far famed in the North. They all lie upon one sandhill, and each of them is more than 215 feet in diameter. The most easterly of them, called in modern times "Woden's barrow," was opened in the years 1846–7 in the following way:—A horizontal passage, 5 feet broad and 7 feet high was cut from one side to the middle of the barrow. The passage was lined with timber and kept open till 1858, when it began to fall in. In 1860 it had to be filled up. The lower part of the barrow is formed by the sandhill itself, but the rest was raised by human labour; it chiefly consists of sand. In the middle there is a round heap of loose stones, 49 feet in diameter. A part of this heap covered the remains of the pyre where the body had been burnt. Right at the bottom of the heap was found a hard compressed layer (6 feet in diameter) of ashes, charcoal, and burnt bones. Four inches deep below this layer was a plain earthenware urn imbedded in sand and covered by a thin slab of stone. It was surrounded by a circle of large stones to protect it from the enormous pressure of the stone heap and mass of sand. It was 8 inches high and 10 inches wide, and was filled to the brim with burnt bones. In the urn and in the great layer of bones above were also

Fig. 144.—Part of a helmet made of iron overlaid with bronze. Upl. ¼.

found relics of several objects injured by the heat of the funeral pyre, such as bronze ornaments, glass beads, bone combs, draughts, also of bone, iron nails, and two pieces of gold ornaments decorated with unusually fine filigree work, &c. The most westerly of the three barrows, "Thor's barrow," as it is called, was opened in 1874, and proved very like in its contents to "Woden's barrow," except that the pile of stones was smaller, and the bones were not preserved in an earthen vessel. Among the things found in Thor's barrow we may notice especially a small cameo of late Roman work (Guide, Fig. 127). The ornaments found in both these barrows show that the graves belong to the first part of the Later Iron Age.

Before the end of this period not only Götaland and Sveneland, but also the coast-land of Norrland as far north as Medelpad was inhabited. The period is an interesting transition between the Earlier Iron Age and the Viking Period. As regards the typical forms of implements, &c., it forms an immediate continuation of the earlier, and a precursor of the later, period. With the latter it has many points of contact, as we see in the forms of sword-hilts, ornamentations, &c. (cf. Figs. 141 and 174). One of the typical forms most characteristic of the last part of the Iron Age, the large oval buckles (Fig. 154), were developed out of the small buckles of the same form (Fig. 145) already found during the period of which we have been speaking.

FIG. 145.—Small oval *fibula* of gilded bronze. Öl. ¼.

D.—The Second Part of the Later Iron Age, or the Viking Period.

(From the beginning of the Eighth to the last half of the Eleventh Century.)

The last part of the Iron Age includes very nearly the same centuries as what is properly known as the Viking Period. It is certainly true that, even before the eighth century, we can speak of, or at any rate suppose, " viking expeditions," if this expression is intended to cover all expeditions by sea made for the purpose of war and plunder. But history has hardly anything to tell us of such early expeditions from Sweden; and they must have been certainly in general confined to the Baltic or the lands of the North. They cannot have had the same importance in the history of the world as those of the northern sea-kings whose ambition drove them to attack the lands of old civilisation of the west and south of Europe. It was in the year 787, according to the *Anglo-Saxon Chronicle*, that a "viking-ship" from the North first appeared off the coasts of England.

The sources of Swedish history during the Viking Period are very meagre, although the time lies only a thousand years back. We have no native chronicles dating from heathen times, or from the first few centuries after the introduction of Christianity. Of history before Olaf Skötkonung we have nothing but one or two short, late, and therefore untrustworthy records of the line of kings. The runic inscriptions, so important for knowing the early language of the country, do not teach us much of its *political history*. We are therefore, as far as literary evidence is concerned, obliged to fall back almost entirely upon what we can get from foreign sources. Among these the Icelandic "Sagas,"[1] as they are called, hold the first rank. In making use of these accounts of heathen times in Sweden, we must not forget that they were not composed in their present form till 250 years after the baptism of Olaf Skötkonung, and also that they should be used with a degree of caution because of their foreign origin.

When we come, on the other hand, to study the *civilisation* of the ancient Swedes, their home-life during the last centuries of heathendom, we are helped by the more perfect knowledge we possess of the state of affairs in Norway and in Iceland at the same time; because the conditions of life seem to have been much alike in different Northern countries. This is particularly true of their faith and religion, as we know by many direct proofs. Though the *Edda*[2] was never in its completeness written down or preserved except in

---

[1] By saga was formerly meant much the same as we now call history, that is to say, a description of events which once happened, not of such as were only the offspring of the writer's fancy.

[2] Or more strictly speaking *Eddas*. "The earlier Edda," or the so-called "Sæmund's Edda," is in its present form a collection, made in 1240, of old songs telling us of our forefathers' faith and practice, and stories of their heroes. One MS. of this long-forgotten collection, almost the only one yet found, was discovered about 1640 in the house of an Icelandic peasant-farmer. "The later Edda," or "Snorri's Edda," is a description of the heathen Northmen's religion and views of the world, and also of their poetry. It was composed by Snorri Sturleson about 1230. [The contents of these Eddas are given in the *Corpus Poeticum Boreale*, Vigfusson and Powell. Tr.]

Iceland; yet everything points to the fact that it once belonged to the whole of the North, indeed probably to the whole of the Teutonic stem, and that the Icelanders merely saved from destruction this common treasure of ancient songs and ancient lore.

As the development of the race may be considered to have gone on generally from worse to better, we get a very fair idea of their life in former days by knowing their condition at later periods. To do so we must take account of many features which by their very simplicity, if nothing else, prove themselves to be relics from heathen times.

The most important source of our knowledge of Swedish civilisation during the Viking Period lies however in the numerous ancient relics and antiquities of this time which are still preserved.

The Svithiod of the Viking Period did not comprise the whole of modern Sweden. Skåne and Halland belonged to Denmark, Bohuslan and Jämtland to Norway, Dalsland and Vermland were disputed border-provinces. The coast-land of Norrland as far as the district of Skellefte was certainly, as the numerous old barrows show, inhabited during the Viking Period, but its population was certainly much thinner than in the South. Finland had not yet been joined to Sweden.

The "lands," as they were then called, which at the end of the heathen times were under tribute to the King of Svithiod, were as follows: the strip of coast which we just mentioned belonging to Norrland, the three provinces round the Mälar Lake, Dalarne, Nerike, Vester-Götland, Öster-Götland, Småland,

Bleking, and the islands of Öland and Gotland.[1] The surface of old Svithiod comprised only about 61,000 English square miles, or a little more than half of the Sweden of the present day, if we exclude the 44,000 square miles of Swedish Lapland.

The appearance of the country has undergone very important changes during the thousand years which separate us from the first century of the Viking Period. Very much of what is now the most fertile ground was then lake or marshy bog, and many parts were navigable during the Middle Ages, or even later, where we can now walk dryshod. This change has not been altogether nature's work. Man has contributed largely to this result by cutting down the forests and by draining the fens, and, during the present century especially, by bringing many new lands into cultivation where these once lay.

How great the population of Svithiod was at the end of heathen times we do not know of course; but we may reasonably suppose that it was not a fifth part so large as that of the Sweden of to-day.

Most of the villages and farms in which the Swedes of the Later Iron Age dwelt had then the same names and the same situations as at the present day. We have a proof of this in the remarkable fact that by almost every village the graves still lie where the heathen population was buried. Before antiquaries were able to get that wide knowledge of antiquities which we now possess, they believed that every collec-

---

[1] That both these islands and Bleking were already considered as belonging to Sweden, we know from the interesting account given by Othere and Wulfstan to King Alfred the Great of their journey to Scandinavia at the end of the ninth century.

tion of ancient barrows or of memorial stones signified a battle-field. But this view became untenable when it was found how numerous these burial-places are, and it had to be given up entirely when so many graves of women and children were found in the "giant-barrows." Many runic stones from the end of heathen times tell us not only the name of the village, but also the owner of the land. Thus Gida, on a stone raised near Ekolsund to her husband Thordjerf Gudlögsson, describes to us how she dwelt at Harvistam, the present Härfvesta. Other stones speak of Ulf of Skalibri (Skålhamra), Björn of Kranbi (Granby), Ågöt of Kalfstadhum, &c. Again, a rich yeoman named Jarlabanki has described on no less than five different stones how "he alone owned the whole of Täby" (in Täby parish, Upland). That many of the present names of places in Sweden date from heathen times is also clear from the fact that several of them are derived from the names of heathen gods, for example, Odensvi, Thorslunda, Frövi, and others, which still mark the spots where men once offered to the Åsa-gods.

We find the following towns already mentioned during the Viking Period: Lödöse on the river Göta-elf, the Göteborg (Gothenburg) of that day, but situated higher up the river; Skara, Faluköping (*sic*), the chief places in the earliest inhabited part of Vester-Götland; Kalmar, Telge, Birka (upon the Björkö in the Mälar Lake), and Sigtuna. We must not however form exaggerated notions of the size of these towns, their population, or the character of their houses.

In the north part of Björkö considerable remains of the old Birka are still visible. The spot where the town lay is still called *by-stán*, or "the place of the town," *by* having this meaning in old Swedish as in Danish. The same spot is also known as *Svarta Jorden* (" the black earth "), because the soil is there full of charcoal and ashes. Among these are found not only domestic utensils, ornaments, and weapons that have been lost or thrown away as rubbish, but also a prodigious number of animal bones, which by the treatment they have evidently received are clearly the relics of the former inhabitants' meals. The view once commonly held that the black earth was a proof that the town was destroyed by fire has been shown to be quite incorrect by means of the very thorough examination to which the place has recently been subjected.[1] It is true that some traces of destructive fires were discovered; but as a rule the colour of the earth comes from the heaps of charcoal and ashes taken from the hearths of the houses, together with bones and other relics of meals. " The black earth " is therefore something like the " kitchen-middens " described at the beginning of this work, although on a much larger scale. Altogether it forms a layer of 3 to 8 ft. upon a surface of about 20 acres. This gives us the size of the ancient town; seen from that point of view the surface might be called rather small than otherwise.

The town was fortified. We still see on the east side a long wall broken by openings for the gates; and doubtless this also surrounded the south side, though there it has been long ago levelled to make way for agriculture. Probably the wall extended to a fortress situated on a hill west of the town, which afforded a last resort in case of siege. This fortress is formed by a wall inclosing the hill except

[1] By Dr. Stolpe, of the National Historical Museum.

upon one side, where it is so steep as to require no defence. The wall is unlike those ancient fortifications which occur in great numbers in the district of the Mälar Lake, in that it is not formed only of loose stones piled together, but, like that surrounding the town itself, seems to have been made of earth, while the inside consists chiefly of loose stones.

Round the town there is a large number of barrows, probably the largest found in any part of Sweden. The number of graves on the island now visible is about 2,100, and yet many have doubtless disappeared in course of time. To these we must also add several graves not covered with a barrow, in which those inhabitants of Birka were buried who, as we gather from history, were converted to Christianity by Ansgar and the missionaries who followed him. We can see that these are Christian graves from the crosses and crucifixes found in them. More than a thousand graves on Björkö have been recently opened and carefully examined, and their contents, like those of "the black earth," prove them to belong to the last part of heathendom, though nothing has been found which can be referred with certainty to a date after 1000 A.D. We may therefore conclude that the town was destroyed by that time.

On this and the neighbouring islands very many Arabic and West-European coins have been found, and also many other things which have come from distant lands, such as vessels, silver and bronze ornaments, &c., from Russia, Gotland, Skåne, Germany, and England. These confirm the statements of ancient writers concerning the active communication between Birka and these countries.

The houses, even at this time, were certainly without exception made of wood; the arts of burning lime and of making bricks were probably first introduced into the North with Christianity. The Swedish dwellings during the Viking Period were undoubtedly like those described in the Northern Sagas; indeed we still occasionally see in out-of-the-way places houses of exactly the same kind, called *ryggås-stugor*, relics of an ancient style of building. In the *Svarta Jorden* on Björkö just mentioned, some curious relics of the burnt houses were discovered, which point to two different sorts of building. On the one hand they found pieces of red-burnt clay, with which the beams of the timber-built houses were tightened after they had been stuffed up with moss, and on the other burnt pieces of clay marked with the impression of laths, and belonging to buildings erected after the manner of the plastered houses of Skåne.

A house of this sort consisted chiefly of a single long four-sided room. The long side-walls were very low, and without windows or doors. The entrance was by one of the gable ends, through an anteroom, and the window (or windows) were in the usually high-pitched roof. This rested upon beams which went right across the house from one wall to the other. The space between the beams was not generally filled up by a ceiling, but admitted the little light which could come through the window and the smoke-hole; for there was no chimney, merely an opening in the top of the roof, by which the smoke escaped from the fire blazing on the middle of the floor. The roof was on the outside covered with turf, thatch, or shingles. If the room was required to be very large, the roof was made to rest upon two rows of upright posts just like the rows of pillars in our churches.

The windows were originally open places in the roof, provided only with a wooden shutter, by which they could be closed. At best they were covered with a thin, more or less transparent substance, probably most frequently consisting of the thin membrane or caul which surrounds the new-born calf. This is still used for windows in some parts of Iceland. Glass windows, although already used by the Romans, certainly were unknown in the North in heathen times.

The walls inside were generally bare or only covered with shields, weapons, and the like; on high festivals they were decked for the occasion with coloured woven hangings.

The floor was composed, as is still the case in many places, of nothing but hard-beaten clay. It could scarcely have been boarded so long as there was no proper fireplace and the fire blazed freely on a hearth composed of flat stones laid on the middle of the floor. The use of built-up fire-places and hearth-stones did not begin in Norway till the end of the eleventh century. This improvement, which must have conduced so largely to domestic comfort, probably did not find its way into Sweden any earlier.

The furniture in the heathen Northman's home was neither much nor costly. Benches and beds fixed to the walls, long tables in front, a few chests for keeping the household treasures—these were the most important things, if not all. "Stools" are however mentioned, as in Hávamál[1]: and in an Icelandic Saga it is related how a man in the year 1011 broke into a barrow in Norway,

[1] See *Corp. Bor.*, vol. i., p. 24. Tr.]

and thereupon found its occupant seated on a stool. Strangely enough, at the end of last century, in opening another Norwegian barrow, two fully-clad skeletons were found in the grave, sitting on wooden stools, which however fell to pieces directly they were exposed to the air.

In the Norwegian yeoman's home, as the Sagas describe it, the place of honour for the father of the house was on the "high seat" in the middle of one of the long walls. In front of the "high seat" stood the two "high-seat-posts." These were dedicated to the gods in heathen times. The existence of such "high seats" in the houses of the Swedish yeoman during heathen times is shown from the fact that both the name and the thing itself continued in some districts till very late times.

The benches were used not only for sitting by day, but in many places they served also for beds by night. We read however also of beds behind the benches. The latter were usually in the better houses laid with rugs or stuffed cushions.[1]

The tables were long and narrow. They did not remain always in front of the benches, but were put out before meals, and usually taken away after, before drinking began in earnest, as we see from many accounts in the Sagas. In a few places in Norway very old tables of this kind have been preserved to quite recent times;

---

[1] In a barrow at Mammen in Jutland was found some years ago "the body of a man resting upon down cushions; of these there are now preserved in the museum at Copenhagen a case made of woollen stuff sewn together, and a quantity of down or feathers tightly pressed and showing clearly the impression of the bones." At about the same time a similar find was made in a Norwegian barrow.

they have often rings by which they were hung up on the walls.

As early as in the *Edda*, we read of chests "rich with jewels." Of these chests we cannot of course expect to find any traces, except those parts which were of metal, such as locks and keys (Fig. 146) and decorative plates. Similar finds have been frequently made in Sweden.

The keys were worn by the mistress of the house as a symbol of her authority indoors. The *Edda* relates how—when Thor had to borrow Freya's clothes in order to get back by craft the hammer stolen from him by the giant—"they dress up Thor in linen and the great Brising-ornament: keys jingle at his belt."[1]

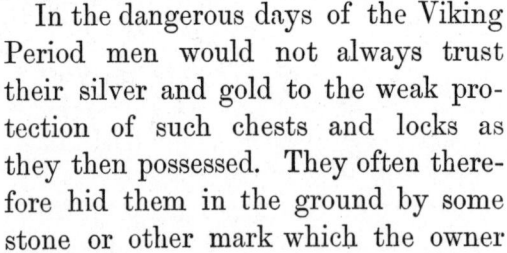

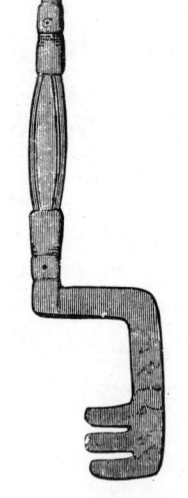

Fig. 146.—Bronze key. Gotl. ⅜.

In the dangerous days of the Viking Period men would not always trust their silver and gold to the weak protection of such chests and locks as they then possessed. They often therefore hid them in the ground by some stone or other mark which the owner only knew. When he died without the opportunity or the wish to reveal the hiding place to any one else, the treasure remained in the ground; and many such hoards have only in our own day been again accidentally brought to light by the plough or the hoe. They were usually deposited in a copper box, a horn, or some such thing, and are often very valuable. Every

[[1] See *Corp. Bor.*, vol. i., p. 178. Tr.]

THE IRON AGE.

year several are discovered, and a large number are now preserved in the National Museum at Stockholm.[1]

During the long winter evenings the room or hall was lighted up chiefly by the fire on the hearth or the torches made of dry cloven pieces of resinous pine and stuck into the walls. At a time when the evenings were not employed in reading and writing, people did not want such good light as now.

By the help of the finds and Sagas we can get a very fair idea of the domestic utensils which the Northmen used during the last few centuries of heathendom. In particular a large number of vessels of different kinds have been preserved to our own day. The cooking vessels were sometimes made of bronze or earthenware; sometimes they were pots made of stone or iron

---

[1] Such hoards from the last few centuries of the Iron Age, generally of silver, have been found in almost all parts of Sweden, but mostly in the neighbourhood of the Mälar Lake, in Skåne, Öland, and especially Gotland. In Svarta Jorden (see above p. 147) in Björkö a hoard of silver was found in 1872 weighing many pounds. In the spot called Följhagen, near the monastery at Roma in Gotland, a copper vessel was found in 1866 containing a large number of ornaments (see Figs. 162—169) and silver coins, together weighing nearly 9 lbs., as well as a little gold ingot. Another hoard which was found twenty years ago near Visby in Gotland contained two gold bracelets weighing 7 oz., and silver ornaments weighing 10 lbs. Another hoard was found more than 40 years ago in Rohne parish (also in Gotland) which weighed nearly 10 lbs. The two largest hoards of this sort which have come to light of late years were found—the one in 1866 at Johannishus at Bleking; the other in 1880 at Espinge in Hurfva parish, Skåne. The first was a copper box containing a large number of perfect and broken ornaments, &c., as well as more than 4,000 silver coins, weighing together 13 lbs. 12 oz. The second comprised nearly 7,000 perfect, and more than 1,700 broken coins, besides ornaments, &c.; they were all of silver, and weighed 19 lbs. 4 oz.

(see p. 139). Frying-pans with handles and gridirons have also been found.

But still more abundant than kitchen-ware are drinking and table vessels, most of them of wood or baked earthenware, but some of them of silver or glass. (Fig. 147.) The earthen vessels were never glazed. In the National Museum there is a beautiful round silver

FIG. 147.—Glass cup. Upl. ½.

bowl (*Ant. suéd*, Fig. 651), ornamented with animal interlacings, which show, by their perfect resemblance to the runic stones, that the work must be Swedish. The bowl was found at Lilla Valla, in Ruthe parish in Gotland, together with a large number of German and English silver coins, of which the latest were struck during the eleventh century.

The ordinary drinking vessel was however the horn, which was generally used even during the Earlier Iron

Age (see p. 112). There is preserved in the National Museum a little silver figure, representing a woman holding a drinking horn in her hand (Fig. 148). We read in the Sagas that it was the custom during the Viking Age for the daughters of the house to hand round the horns to the men as they drank.

At meal-times the tables were laid with cloths, at any rate in the houses of the rich, as we see from the *Edda* song *Rigsthula*, which has a simple but vivid description of Heimdal's visit to the home where the ancestor of the *jarls* was afterwards born :—[1]

FIG. 148.—Silver pendant. Öl. ¼.

> Then took the mother
> The embroidered cloth
> Of linen, white,
> And laid it on the board.
> Then set she down
> Thin loaves of bread,
> Wheaten, white,
> Upon the cloth.
> Next brought she forth
> Dishes brimfull,
> Silver-mounted,
> High-flavoured ham
> And roasted fowl.
> There was wine in cans,
> Beauteous cups.
> They drank, they talked
> Till break of day,
>   &c., &c.

The dishes, or plates, upon which the food was served, were indeed usually simple wooden trenchers; though

[1] See *Corp. Bor.*, vol. i., p. 239. Tr.]

sometimes, as in the verses just quoted, we have descriptions of such as were, partly at any rate, of silver. But none of the kind from the Viking Period have been discovered in Swedish finds. Pewter plates were probably still quite unknown. The food was cut with the common knives which every one carried at their belts.[1] Forks are the invention of a later day; during the heathen times men used their fingers, and therefore Northmen, like the Greeks of Homer's poems, washed their hands before and after meals. The spoons were made of wood, horn, or bone (Fig. 149); silver spoons have not yet been discovered in any *Swedish* find belonging to heathen times (but see p. 112).

It is certainly difficult for us to imagine how people contrived to get along at a time when they had neither potatoes, coffee, tea, sugar, nor any of the spices of the

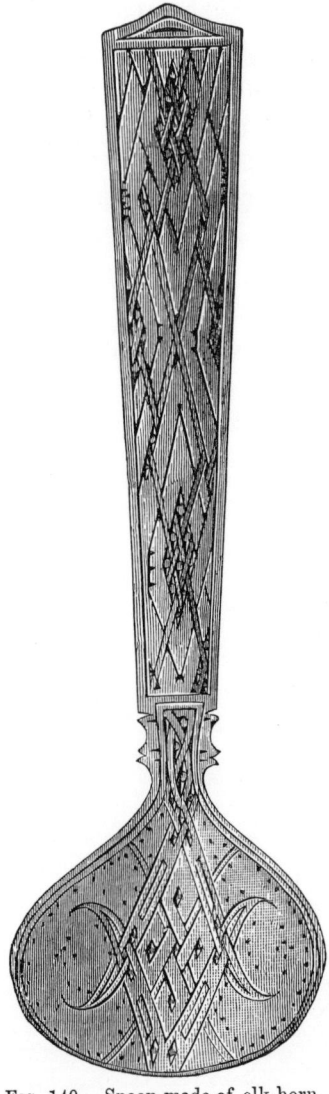

FIG. 149.—Spoon made of elk-horn. Upl. ¼.

[[1] Knives are still so worn by the peasants in Sweden, Norway, and Finland.—Tr.]

South. But they had bread instead of potatoes, milk instead of coffee and tea, honey instead of sugar, and the appetite which comes from hard work is always the best spice. Besides the field and dairy produce, there was plenty of wild game, and several finds have proved that they had both geese and poultry at this time.

Snorri relates of King Sigurd Syr, the step-father of St. Olaf, who dwelt at Ringerike in Norway, that the guests in his house got every other day fish and milk, and on alternate days meat and ale.[1] Mead was a costly drink, and was not produced on ordinary occasions, and peculiar herbs were sometimes added to make it more intoxicating. Wine was not unknown, but seems to have been very scarce.

We can get very clear ideas about the dress of the Northmen at this time from the Eddas, the Sagas, and the finds. The accounts of the Sagas must however in this respect be used with great caution, because they were not written down till some two centuries after the end of heathendom, when important changes had taken place in the matter of dress. In many cases it is difficult therefore to decide whether the writer of the Saga was describing a faithfully preserved tradition, or was clothing his heroes in the fashion of a later time. We have no such violence to "historical costume" to fear in the contemporary representations and the finds in the barrows of heathen times.

Many finds prove that besides skins and furs, woollen, linen, and silken stuffs were used by the Northmen during the Viking Age. Silken stuffs were however of course a great luxury. In *Rigsthula* we read that the new-

[1] See Laing's *Sea-Kings*, vol. ii., p. 31.—Tr.

158   ANCIENT SWEDISH CIVILISATION.   [CHAP.

born jarl was wrapt in silk;[1] and in the barrow at Mammen in Jutland already mentioned there was found a well-preserved belt, &c. of silk ornamented with silver and gold. In the same find there was also a woollen

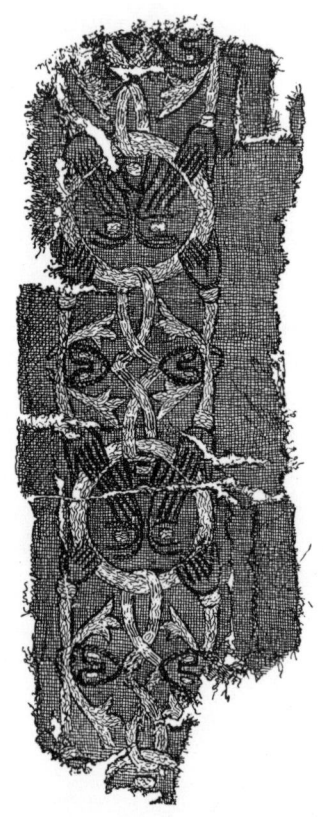

FIG. 150.—Piece of a woollen mantle with embroidery. Denmark ⅓.

mantle with embroidered work representing a man's face, a lion, a beautiful leafy tendril, &c. (Figs. 150 and 151). It is not however yet certain whether these

[1 See *Corp. Bor.*, vol. i., p. 240, line 130.—Tr.]

pieces of ornamental work were produced in the North, or brought thither from foreign lands.

On the other hand the ordinary woollen and linen materials were generally the productions of native industry. This is seen, among other things, by the

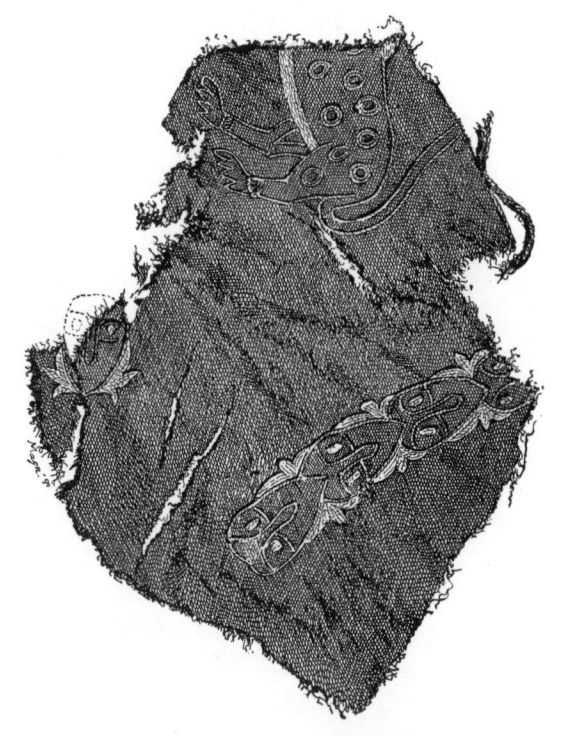

FIG. 151.—Piece of a woollen mantle with embroidery   Denmark ⅓.

relics of the instruments employed in making them, which are often contained in the Northern finds of this Age. For instance, we have sometimes found the hackles used in preparing flax and the weights by which the warp was kept stretched in the loom. We cannot of course expect that any other parts of looms and the like, of this Age, except what was made of stone or metal, could defy the ravages of time; yet the ancient forms of distaffs and looms preserved down to historic times, and in some distant parts to our own day, show how the women of the North spun and wove a thousand

FIG. 152.—A loom from the Färö Isles.

years ago (see Fig. 152). The spinning-wheel, which is now in towns looked upon merely as a relic of the past, was probably yet unknown. They used the distaff instead, just as the Grecian women of whom Homer sang did two thousand years before, and just as the girls do still in the remotest parts of Dalarna. Small spinning-whorls of stone, sometimes of amber, exactly like those used in these distaffs of Dalarna, are also often met with in Swedish finds of this time.

We are helped in forming an idea of the domestic life and occupations of these ancient times by a verse in *Rigsthula,* which describes a visit of Rig to a good couple, representing the gentry of the period. We see from this that the women of quality in those days were not superior to active household work.[1]

> The father sat
> and twined his bowstring,
> bent elm for bow
> and hafted arrows.
> But the housewife thought
> of handiwork,[2]
> Smoothed her linen
> and pleated her sleeves.

The men's dress comprised in the main the same parts as that of the present day: a shirt, breeches, stockings, shoes, a coat ("kirtle," as it was called), kept together by a belt, and over this a cloak or mantle, and upon the head a cap or hat. These different articles of dress were often made of brilliant colours, but their shape was usually the same as now. The kirtle does not seem to have been open in front, as coats are now usually worn; and so was probably much like a long blouse. The cloak was usually fastened with a buckle.

This description is gathered, it is true, mostly from the Icelandic Sagas; but that it applies also to Sweden is shown, among other things, by the representations of Swedish dresses found on many runic stones belonging to the end of heathen and the beginning of Christian

[1] See *Corp. Bor.*, vol. i., p. 239.—Tr.]
[2] See note in *Corp. Bor.*, vol. i., p. 519.—Tr.]

times. We find them, for example, upon a stone at Hunestad in Skåne, on both sides of a stone in the churchyard at Leberg in Öster-Götland, upon a stone now built into Fernebo church in Gestrikland, and upon some of the runic so-called "picture-stones" (*Bildstenar*) in the island of Gotland. We have an interesting contribution to our knowledge of the Swedish dress at the beginning of the Viking Period in the remarkable figures upon four bronze plates found in 1870 in a cairn at

FIG. 153.—Bronze plate with figures in relief. Öl. ¼.

Björnhofda in Öland, and now preserved in the National Museum (Fig. 153.)

In order to give a more vivid picture of the dress of the time in question, we will quote the description of the clothes which King Sigurd Syr in Ringerike wore when he went out over the fields and superintended the harvest.[1] This was in the autumn of 1014, on the occasion when his stepson Olaf Haraldsson, better known perhaps as St. Olaf, came to visit him. "It is thus said

[[1] See *Sea-Kings*, vol. ii., p. 27.—Tr.]

of his (Sigurd's) attire," so writes Snorri, "that he had a blue kirtle and blue hosen, high boots bound about the legs, a gray cloak and a gray hat, a shade about the

Fig. 154.—Oval bronze brooch. Öl. ½.

face, and in his hand a staff, which had at the top a silver knob overlaid with gold, and in it a silver ring." In order to do due honour to his stepson, he had "his boots taken off, and set upon his feet hosen of cordwain, and bound upon them gilded spurs ; then took he off his cloak and kirtle, and clad him in his gala clothes, and over all a scarlet cloak, and girt about him a decorated sword, and set upon his head a gilded helmet and mounted on his horse, which had a gilded saddle and a bridle all-gilded and set with melted stones (that is, enamel)." A bridle with gilt mountings and

FIG. 155.—Round bronze brooch. Ångermanl $\frac{1}{4}$.

FIG. 156.—Round silver brooch. Gotl. $\frac{1}{4}$.

enamelled bronze exactly corresponding to the description of that belonging to Sigurd's horse was found in one of the graves near the church at Vendel already mentioned (see p. 139).

The women's dress seems to have been much like that still worn in country places.

A visit to the National Museum in Stockholm—so rich in costly memorials of the Viking Period especially —will show, better than any words can do, how true the accounts are which the Sagas give us when they

III.]   THE IRON AGE.   165

speak of the luxury and magnificence which the Northmen of both sexes were able to develop a thousand years ago. We see the handsome and as a rule very tastefully wrought brooches and buckles of silver and bronze, the latter often ornamented with plates and

FIG. 157.   Silver brooch.   Ö.-Götl. ½.

twists of gold or silver; belts and torques of massive silver; bracelets and finger-rings of gold and silver, solid and sometimes very heavy; chains and pendants for the neck and breast of gold, silver, and bronze; large and handsome beads of silver, glass, glass mosaic, rock crystal, carnelian, amber, &c.; bone combs often of very fine workmanship, &c., &c. (See Figs. 154—169.)

These many kinds of ornaments are not only important because they show us the early Northmen's magnificence; they are of more importance as proving that these so-called "barbarians," so dreaded by the

FIG. 158.—Bronze brooch of silver-gilt. Sk. ¼.

people of Western Europe, should not be regarded merely as wild warriors, but were also well versed in peaceful pursuits.

There was a time when it was said that all Swedish antiquities which showed any artistic skill must have been brought into the country as booty from foreign lands. A calmer inquiry in our own day has shown

III.]   THE IRON AGE.   167

however that most even of the best-worked ornaments are products of native industry. Nay, we have now reason to wonder that there is, as a matter of fact,

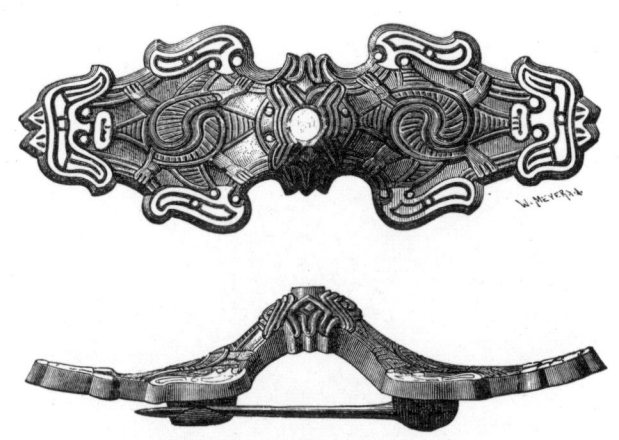

Fig. 159.—Bronze *fibula* (two views). ¼.

Fig. 160.—Ring-shaped bronze brooch. Gotl. ½.

so little found in Sweden which can be supposed to have been brought there by the vikings from Western Europe. If we except the German and Anglo-Saxon coins of the tenth and the beginning of the eleventh centuries, there is little left to remind us of their frequent visits to England, France, and other lands plundered by the Northmen in their "west-viking." The explanation of this somewhat surprising discovery must however be sought partly in the fact that only a very small part of the Northmen's booty has come into our hands, partly that a large proportion of the

FIG. 161.—Solid silver bracelet. Gotl. ¼.

metal ornaments &c. brought back by the returning sea-kings were worked up again in course of time. To this we must add that many vikings remained behind in foreign lands, and that many ships either foundered as they were returning home, or were seized —booty and all—by some stronger foe.

In the barrows of this time we often find a number of tools, such as anvils, sledges, hammers, pincers (Figs. 170 and 171), files, awls, borers, axes, knives, planes, scrapers, and saws. The larger anvils were made of stone, the smaller of iron. We also find bellows

III.]   THE IRON AGE.   169

FIG. 162.—Twisted silver bracelet. Gotl. ¼.

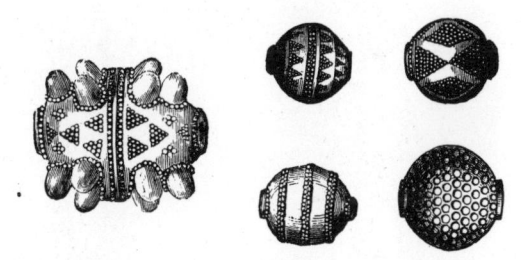

FIGS. 163—167. Silver beads. Gotl. ¼.

FIG. 168.—Silver pendant.   FIG. 169.—Silver pendant.
        Gotl. ¼.   Gotl. ¼.

FIGS. 162—169.—SILVER ORNAMENTS FOUND AT FÖLHAGEN, NEAR ROMA, IN
                    GOTLAND.

170 ANCIENT SWEDISH CIVILISATION. [CHAP.

and many other tools represented on the wonderful "Sigurd's carving" (*Sigurdsristningen*) in Södermanland, to which we shall shortly have occasion to refer.

We have an interesting relic belonging to a smith of this period in the hoard found twenty years ago in the parish of Eke in Gotland; it is now preserved in the

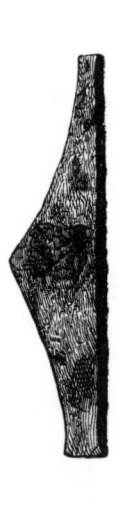

FIG. 170.—Iron hammer.
Smål. ⅓.

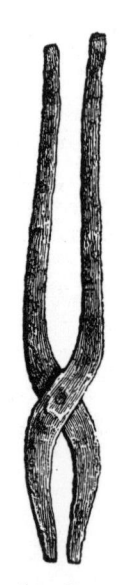

FIG. 171.—Iron pincers.
Södermanl. ⅛.

National Museum. It was discovered by men who were cutting a dyke, and comprised the following articles :—
A large pair of tongs and two large iron weights, a strong hook belonging probably to a pair of scales, two small bronze moulds used either for casting or relief work, three small bronze buckles (Guide Fig. 155) still joined together (which had been cast in the same mould,

and were evidently in the same condition exactly as when they left it), several other buckles, keys, &c., of bronze and iron. Of these some seemed to have been worn out and had probably been collected for working up again; while others were only half prepared, and may therefore, like the three buckles mentioned above, be regarded as specimens of the smith's skill, who for some reason unknown to us buried these things in the ground.[1]

As far as the raw material is concerned we have good reason to believe that most of the metal was imported from other countries. It is however very probable that even during heathen times the Swedes understood the art of smelting the metal obtained from ferruginous deposits. A large quantity of ore obtained from such deposits in pools and lakes is smelted at the present day in Sweden. But it is hardly likely that before the introduction of Christianity they began to work any of the Swedish iron-mines.

In order to smelt the ore thus obtained they probably then knew only of what were afterwards called the "heathen-blowers" (*hedningebläster*), or the same method which is still used in the northern parts of Dalarna and Härjeådalen, and seems to be also in vogue in Finland and central Russia. In small pits or ovens built up of stone and clay the ore was melted down with the help of ordinary bellows into small

[1] It may perhaps be here worth noticing that the farm on which the hoard was found is called Smiss—that is, "Smith's (farm)". It is of course possible that this is merely a coincidence, but it is also possible that the farm got this name because a smith —or perhaps several smiths in succession (the occupation being handed on from father to son)—dwelt there during the heathen times.

ingots known as "Osmund's iron." In several places in the country traces of this method of working iron during the heathen times are said to have been found.

The word "smith" at that time was used of any man who was skilful in working metals. The Sagas certainly speak of the dwarfs as remarkably skilled in smith's work, but they also tell us that there were smiths of a more human type, and that these were highly respected. We can see this even so early as in the Saga of Völund (or German Wieland) [1] and from the fact that one of the freeborn yeoman's sons in *Rigsthula* is called Smith; [2] the name is also found on some runic stones, as, for example, upon that at Gårdby Church in Öland. Again the Icelandic Sagas tell us of several kings and other mighty men who understood the art of making their own weapons. Skallagrim, the far-famed father of Egil, one of the most renowned Icelanders of his time, stood himself in his smithy and "hammered the iron."

We are too much disposed to attribute to the ancient Northmen an exclusive devotion to the enticing adventures and easy spoils of pillage, and are apt to imagine that they altogether despised the quiet business of a peaceful life, leaving it to thralls who were unworthy of taking part in the fray. This idea is entirely contradicted by what we know of the conditions of life during the Viking Period. As a proof of this we

[1 See *Corp. Bor.*, vol. i., p. 169. English readers will call to mind the so-called "Weyland Smith's cave," near the White Horse on the Berkshire Downs, and the legends connected with it.—Tr.]

[2 *Id.*, vol. i., p. 238.—Tr.]

need but adduce the description in the *Edda* of the free-born yeoman's son :[1]

> He now learnt
> to tame oxen
> and till the ground,
> to timber houses
> and build barns,
> to make carts
> and form ploughs.

And Snorri tells of the already mentioned King Sigurd Syr in Ringerike,[2] that the messenger who came to tell him of Olaf's unexpected arrival found the king out in the field, where he had "many men, of whom some cut the corn, others laid it in stacks and barns. The king and two men with him went sometimes into the field, sometimes to where the corn was being gathered in." This shows how honourable the work was thought.

Pasturage and tillage furnished then, as now, the most important means of subsistence. Long before this, more than 2,500 years before the end of heathendom, almost all the most important domestic animals were, as we have seen, to be found in Sweden, namely dogs, horses, cattle, sheep, goats, and pigs. That of poultry they had now geese and fowls at any rate, we have already mentioned. Life in the cots of Dalarna and Norrland in our own day is doubtless very much like what it was a thousand years ago, with the same simplicity and freshness, the same solitude, fostering the poetical, somewhat imaginative temperament which is so pleasingly expressed in their folk songs.

Bee-culture was considerably practised during heathen

[1 See *Corp. Bor.*, vol. i., p. 238.—Tr.]
[2 See *Sea Kings*, vol. ii., p. 27.—Tr.]

times, because, to say nothing of other uses, much honey was required for mead. Vermland is especially praised for its richness in bees. In a Gotland grave belonging to the end of this period a beautiful *fibula* of gilded bronze was found, in which there was still a piece of wax coloured green by the verdigris from the metal; it is now in the National Museum. With Christianity this industry increased in importance, because wax lights were wanted for the churches.

The most common kind of cereal during the Viking Period was barley; but oats, rye, and a certain amount of wheat were also cultivated. In a verse of the *Rigsthula* already quoted we read of "thin loaves of bread, wheaten white."[1]

Crop-failures and famines were pretty frequent, and the only remedy against them was sought in richer offerings to the angry gods. If nothing else availed, they had recourse to human sacrifices. We remember how we read in the Ynglinga Saga that the Swedes, after the crops had failed for several years in succession, and the gods would not be pacified with meaner victims, at last offered up their king.

Of course not much in the way of agricultural implements has been preserved from heathen times. A few axes, however, as well as plough-shares, sickles (Fig. 172), and scythes have been sometimes found.

FIG. 172.—Iron sickle. Ö-Götl. ¼.

[1] See above p. 155.

Corn was threshed with a flail and was ground, at least generally, in hand mills; this was, as we see from Fjolner's Saga, the work of female thralls.

Certainly mills were often of the same simple kind as during the Stone Age. They consisted namely of a block of stone with a large oval depression in which the corn was crushed by the hand with a round stone. Mills of this kind are often found buried, and seem to have been used till quite lately in distant parts of the country. But that even in heathen times hand-mills [1] of a better construction were known is shown by one of the songs of the *Edda*, the poem of Helgi Hundingsbane.[2] It is related there that Helgi in order to escape his enemies, was obliged to dress up as a female thrall and go out to grind. He does it with such violence that "the stones crack and the barn breaks in pieces." Whereupon one of his enemies says:

> More suited
> to these hands
> is the sword-hilt
> than the "mill-wood" (*i.e.* the handle of the mill).

We know little of any fruit or garden culture during the Viking Period, and there cannot have been much. It was in the Middle Ages, especially inside the still walls of the monastery, that it first flourished. However the Saga of Idun's apples makes it clear that this

[1] Water-mills were used by the Romans during the Empire, but it is difficult to say whether they were known in the North before the introduction of Christianity. They are certainly mentioned in the earliest Swedish MSS., but these are nearly 200 years later than the suppression of heathendom in that country. Wind-mills were probably a much later invention; as far as we know they are first mentioned in Sweden about 1330, or rather later.

[2] See *Corp. Bor.*, vol. i., p. 148.—Tr.]

fruit was not entirely unknown during heathen times, and in one of the songs of the *Edda*, Frey's servant Skirnir says to Gerd the daughter of the giant:[1]

> Apples eleven
> Here have I all-golden,
> Them will I give thee
> to buy thine affection,
> if thou to Frey
> wilt promise thy love.

Besides we often hear of nuts and "nut-groves," where the women used to amuse themselves in the summer time while the men were out hunting.

The chase and sports in the open air were the men's chief delight. The chase, at first arising from the necessity of procuring food, soon became also a pleasure, eagerly pursued in days when men courted danger and loved manly pursuits.

Hawking was practised in heathen times, and the North was then, just as in the Middle Ages, famed for its falcons. It has been even supposed that this knightly sport actually originated in the North, and through the Norman barons spread over Europe. The discovery of a falcon's bones in one of the graves at Vendel has been already mentioned (see p. 139).

Snorri relates of Olaf Skötkonung that he rode out early one day with his hawks and hounds, and with him his men. When they flew the hawks, the king's hawk in one flight brought down two blackcock, and directly after he had another flight and slew three more. The hounds ran below and seized every bird as it fell to the ground; the king rode home well pleased with his quarry. When he rode into the court-yard his daughter

[1] See *Corp. Poet.*, vol. i., p. 113.—Tr.

came and greeted him. He told her at once of his sport, and said, "Have you known of any king who made so big a bag in such a short space?" "A fine morning's sport," she answered, "is this, my lord, in that you have bagged five black-cock; but Olaf king of Norway made a better bag when he took in one morning five kings and laid their kingdoms under his sway." [1]

Among outdoor sports games of ball seems to trace their origin to heathen times. For such games and other manly exercises the young folk would gather from the whole neighbourhood, sometimes meeting on playgrounds specially set apart, as is the case up to the present time in Gotland.

Of musical instruments we read of the lyre, the horn, the pipe, the fiddle, and above all the harp, one of the oldest and most prized. Snorri relates of Olaf Skötkonung, that when the meats were set upon the king's table, the players stepped forth with "harps, fiddles, and other instruments." To the tones of the harp the Skalds generally sang their songs. Skalds often visited at the court of the Swedish kings; sometimes they came from Iceland. Thus we read that when the Icelander Hjälte came from St. Olaf on his well known business to Olaf Skötkonung, he found at the Swedish king's court two of his countrymen, the Skalds Gissur and Ottar.

That the ancient art of poetry was not unknown in Sweden is proved also by the runic inscriptions in verse (in the ancient metre called *fornyrdalag*) which still survive, as for instance that upon a stone at Karlevi in Öland.

Games played with dice were, as we have seen from the grave-finds, already in vogue during the earlier part of

[1 See *Sea-Kings*, vol. ii., p. 108.—Tr.]

the Iron Age (see pp. 114, 138). In graves of the Later Iron Age draughts and dice are found pretty frequently.

Chess too was probably in heathen times already known in the North. It has been thought likely that this much-prized game was brought to Scandinavia from Asia through Constantinople as early as the eighth or ninth century, if not before. Charlemagne seems to have given a costly set of chessmen to the treasury at the monastery of St. Denis. We have also an account of a complete set found in 1730 in an ancient barrow in Hedemark in Norway; unfortunately the pieces, which had been wrapped in a silk cloth, are now no longer preserved. On the other hand we have in the National Museum a small antiquity of bone, which possibly belonged to a set of chessmen. It was found some years ago in a barrow near the church of Salem in Södermanland. In two barrows close by they came across several round draughts made of bone, like those found at Ultuna (see p. 138). Lastly we may call to mind the famous chess-match which was played at Röskilde between King Knut [Canute] the Great and his brother-in-law Ulf Jarl, in 1017, and resulted in the murder of the latter on the following day in the choir of St. Lucius.[1]

But more popular than either chase or games were the wild pleasures of the battle-field. The Northmen actually believed that the joys of Valhalla after death would consist in mighty conflicts by day, and that when the battle was ended both fallen and victorious would every evening enjoy a glad banquet in Woden's Hall.

Sagas and songs are full of accounts of battles and exploits which should secure the hero's name an un-

[[1] See *Sea-Kings*, vol. ii. pp. 252-3.—Tr.]

dying honour. We cannot now stop to describe these exploits, but will just cast a glance at the weapons which once made the Northmen so terror-inspiring. The abundant finds and many different accounts in the Sagas give us a clearer knowledge on this than on many other points.

As defensive weapons we find mentioned coats of mail, helmets, and shields. Coats of mail skilfully made of fine iron rings already occur, as we have seen, during the Earlier Iron Age (see Fig. 110). In the rich Norman embroidery of the time of William the Conqueror, known as the Bayeux Tapestry, we see similar coats of mail worn by the Norman knights at the Battle of Hastings in 1066. According to Grimnismal, one of the songs in the *Edda*, the benches in Woden's Hall were covered with mail.[1] Besides coats of mail we read in the Nothern Sagas also of defensive armour made of leather, thick linen, and the like.

The helmets found at Ultuna and Vendel (see pp. 138, 139) are the only ones of the Iron Age hitherto found in Sweden. On the bronze plates found at Thorslunda we see helmets decorated with figures of animals (see Fig. 153).

Shield-bosses of iron are not uncommon in the Swedish graves of the Viking Period The shields themselves, which were made of wood, leather, or something else of the kind, have of course almost always perished. We have a remarkable exception to this in the ship found in the barrow near Gokstad, and described below. All round the vessel were set sixty-four shields, most of which are almost perfectly preserved. They were painted alternately yellow and black, and were all

[1] See *Corp. Bor.*, vol. i., p. 71.—Tr.]

round. That they were usually of this shape is shown by such descriptions as "the battle's wheel," "the battle's ring," given them by the Skalds. In the museum at Christiania there is still preserved an old round wooden shield, with an ornamental rim and a runic inscription round the edge of the boss. There is a similar round shield also in the museum at Copenhagen,

FIG. 173.—Iron axe. Upl. ⅓.

with a decorated rim, but without runes. They both belong to the early centuries of the Middle Ages.

The offensive weapons during the Viking Period were swords and spears, battle-axes (Fig. 173) and clubs, bows and arrows. The chief metal was iron, or more strictly speaking, steel; but it was often, for decorative purposes, inlaid with gold or silver. The sword was two-edged, strong, and sharp (Figs. 174, 175); the length of the blade, which was not unfrequently damasked (Fig. 175), was usually about two feet six

III.] THE IRON AGE. 181

inches. The hilts, which were often tastefully inlaid with silver, were usually designed for one hand; the cross-guard was short. One of the most valuable

Fig. 174.—Upper part of a two-edged iron sword. Upl. ½

swords found in Sweden of the Viking Period, probably the last part of it, is one found some years ago in a peat-bog at Dybeck, in Skåne. The cross-guard and pommel consisted of solid silver-gilt with beautiful decorations, and the hilt itself had been tightly bound with gold thread.

The other weapons were much like those belonging to the earlier part of the Iron Age.

Shipbuilding reached a high degree of perfection in the North during the Viking Period, higher perhaps than in most Christian lands; and the numbers of ships in Northern countries must have been very considerable. Fleets of from 600 to 700 ships are frequently mentioned. Snorri even relates that the Danish king Knut the Great for his attack on Norway collected a fleet of "twelve hundred ships."[1] This would mean 1440, because 120 was then reckoned to the hundred.

FIG. 175.—Part of a damasked sword-blade. Boh. ⅓.

Ships were propelled sometimes by a sail, sometimes with oars. On each ship there was generally only one mast and one sail (see Figs. 176—180). The sail, in form much like our modern square-sail, was usually made of wool, and sometimes had blue, red, and green stripes. The number of oars was often very considerable, and the size of a ship-of-war was described by the number of rowing benches. A "twenty-seat" for example, meant a boat with twenty pairs of oars. The "Long Serpent," Olaf Trygvason's famed ship—the largest of the time in Norway—had thirty-four pairs of oars and nearly a thousand men; its keel was 144 feet long.[2] Knut the Great had a ship called "Dragon"

[1 See *Sea-Kings*, vol. ii., p 267.—Tr.]
[2 *Ib.*, vol. i., pp. 456–458.—Tr.]

III.] THE IRON AGE. 183

with as many as sixty pairs.[1] Usually all the oars were in one row: but Erling Skacke in Norway caused a ship

FIG. 176.—Grave-stone with carvings and runic inscription, from Tjängvide. Gotl.

to be built in the twelfth century with two banks of oars, one over the other. As in the boats of the Earlier

[[1] See *Sea Kings*, vol. ii, p. 243.—Tr.]

184   ANCIENT SWEDISH CIVILISATION.   [CHAP.

Iron Age the rudder was not directly in the stern, but on the right side near the stern; and hence this side is still called the *star*board.

The ships were generally painted and the gunwale decorated with a row of shields, as we see on Figs. 177 and 180. The stem often ended in a gilded dragon's head, and the stern was sometimes finished off in the

FIG. 177.—A Northman's ship from the end of the eleventh century, taken from the Bayeux tapestry.

form of a dragon's tail; hence ships-of-war were commonly called "dragons." We sometimes find that ships had a dragon's head at both ends, or that the stem was decorated with the gilded head of a man, or of an ox. King Olaf the Saint had for the figure head of his ship "Karl-höfdi," himself carved a man's head (Fig. 177).

Erik Jarl had at the battle of Svolder, in the year 1000, a ship called "Beard," because the stem as far down as the water was covered with iron plates, and

III.]   THE IRON AGE.   185

above had a "beard" consisting probably of iron spikes sticking out.[1]

Before a sea-fight they used to bind the stems, where the chief combatants stood, together, so that every line of ships formed a continuous whole, and they could fight almost as though they were on land. When the ships lay still, especially for the night, they were generally protected by a sort of tent.

By a wonderful conjunction of favourable conditions, we have two Northmen's ships preserved from the

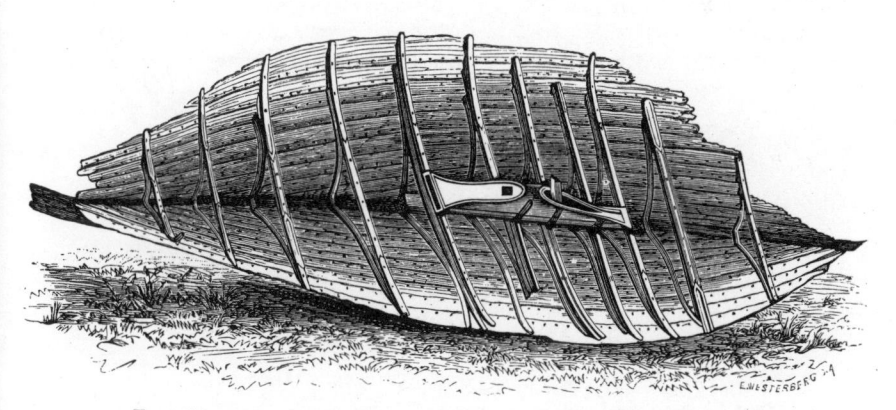

FIG. 178.—An oak ship found in the barrow at Tune in South Norway.

Viking Period to our own day. In 1867 a large barrow was opened at Tune, near Frederikstad, in the south of Norway. A man was there found buried in his ship, with his weapons and two horses. As the lower part of the barrow consisted of blue clay, the greater part of the ship was preserved almost uninjured (see Fig. 178). It is built nearly in the same fashion as that found in the Nydam bog (see p. 115), and, like it, is pointed at both ends but, unlike it, had a mast.

[1] See *Sea-Kings*, vol. i., pp. 473, 474.—Tr.]

Another ship still better preserved was found in 1880, in a large barrow—itself too composed mainly of blue clay—at Gokstad, near Sandefjord, in the south of Norway (Figs. 179, 180). It is seventy-eight feet long, is pointed at both ends, and has a mast and sixteen pairs of oars. As we already observed, it was decorated with shields, thirty-two on each side (see p. 184). In a grave chamber, just behind the mast, the dead chieftain was buried with his weapons; but his rest had been

FIG. 179.—Viking-ship *as found* at Gokstad, in South Norway.

soon disturbed by grave-plunderers. Together with him were buried no less than twelve horses, six dogs, and a peacock. Both these ships are now among the treasures of the museum in Christiania.

All communications between the North and other parts of Europe during the Viking Period were not however of a hostile character. The peaceful enterprises of commerce were engaged in with a vigour which there has been only too much tendency to underrate.

The position of Sweden especially, at a time when the greater part of what are now its western coasts belonged

III.]   THE IRON AGE.   187

to Denmark or Norway, restricted its commerce almost
entirely to the lands on the east and south coasts of
the Baltic. And yet we have abundant means of
proving that at this time the ancient Svithiod, as it
was called, had also both peaceful and warlike relations

FIG. 180.—The Gokstad ship *restored*.

with the lands of Western Europe, and especially the
British Isles.

In Gestrikland, Upland, Vestmanland, Södermanland,
Öster-Götland, and Småland there are a number of
runic stones, which were raised to the memory of men
who had travelled to England. Built up in the wall of
the church at Old Upsala, there is a runic stone which
"Sigvid traveller to England" had caused to be inscribed in memory of his father. Thus Sigvid, we see,
had the good fortune to return home from his travels.
But of others it is expressly said that they died in

England. At Kolstad, in the parish of Häggeby in Upland, there is a runic stone engraved by two sons in memory of their father, who "remained in the West in the *thingalid*," by which is probably meant the beginning of a standing army in England, set on foot by Knut the Great. Another runic stone, at Rösås in Småland, was set up to the memory of one Gunnar, who was "buried in a stone coffin at Bath in England."

We have further traces of the journeys made for the purpose of "plundering in the West" (*vesterviking*), and of commerce with England, in the number of Anglo-Saxon coins of the tenth and eleventh centuries found every year buried in Sweden (Fig. 181).[1] It is possibly true that the greater part of the coins struck by the unfortunate King Æthelræd, who died in 1016, were originally extorted by vikings; but this can hardly be supposed to have been the case with the great quantities of coins, found also in Sweden, which bear the names of the Anglo-Danish kings Knut the Great and Hardaknut, and were struck in England. Even the greater part of Æthelræd's coins must have got by commerce to the places where they are *now* found; for they are comparatively very scarce in the western parts of Scandinavia, although the inhabitants of these took the greatest share in plundering expeditions to England, whereas a surprisingly large number has been found in the districts along the eastern coast of Sweden, and especially Gotland.

We find a proof of English influence on Swedish

[1] We have exact knowledge of at least 25,000 Anglo-Saxon coins found in Sweden, all of silver; to this we should add the great mass of coins which we know to have been found there, especially in earlier times, but the number of which is now unknown.

affairs at this time in the fact that the coins of Olaf Skötkonung (see Fig. 182), the earliest made in the country, were struck exactly after the pattern of contemporary English coins. Further than this, they were struck by minters who had been sent for from England.[1]

A still weightier influence was that exercised by the many English missionaries who contributed so largely to the victory of Christianity in Sweden.

Though we must not therefore overlook the active communication which existed between Sweden and the

FIG. 181.—Anglo-Saxon silver coin of King Æthelræd. Upl. ¼.

FIG. 182.—Earliest Swedish silver coin struck for Olaf Skötkonung. ¼.

west of Europe, we can yet easily see that her closest connexions were then, as many centuries after, with countries lying to the east and south.

Of this too the runic stones bear an eloquent testimony. Many of them were raised to the memory of men, who travelled in "Eastway" (*i.e.*, the lands bordering on the Baltic). Others speak more definitely of travels to Finland, Tavastland [now the central province of Finland], Esthonia, Livonia, Semgallen (the east part of Courland as far as the river Düna), and Holmgård (the modern Novgorod). A large number of runic stones in

[1] On the back of the coin represented in Fig. 182 we read that the minter was Godwine, clearly an English name.

190 ANCIENT SWEDISH CIVILISATION. [CHAP.

Upland, Södermanland, and Öster-Götland speak especially of men who followed Ingvar on his journey eastwards.

Many runic stones tell us of Swedes who set forth on long journeys to the east and south as far as Greece,

FIG. 183.—Marble lion with runic inscription, originally in the Piræus, now at Venice. Height 9 ft.

where many of their countrymen entered service as members of the emperor's body-guard (*väringar*) at Constantinople. The most remarkable of these runic inscriptions is one upon an ancient marble lion, which during the Viking Period stood in the Piræus near Athens, but was brought to Venice in the seventeenth century (see Fig. 183). The chief part of the inscription is certainly illegible, but the form of the interlacing ornaments proves it to have been cut by a Swede.

A runic stone in the parish of Ytter-Sela in Södermanland was raised by Sirid to her husband Sven, who "often sailed with costly ships to Semgallen round Tumisnis." Tumisnis is the present Dumesness, the

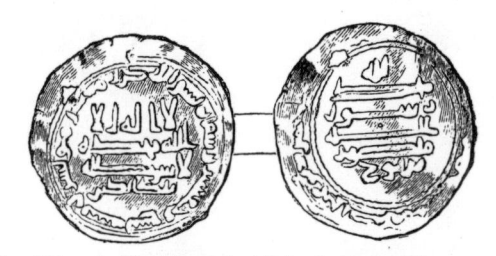

FIG. 184.—Arabic silver coin (*dirhem*) struck at Samarcand in A.D. 903. Gotl. ½.

most northerly point of Courland, whence it begins to trend to the bay of Riga.

Adam of Bremen in speaking of the famous trading-town of Birka upon an island in the Mälar Lake, during the last part of heathen times, relates that "Danes, Northmen, Slavs, Sembers, and other Scythian peoples used to travel thither in their ships."

The astonishing quantity of Arabian coins (Fig. 184) and silver ornaments from the east found in Sweden point to commerce with eastern countries. More than 20,000 Arabian silver coins are known to have been found in Swedish soil; most of them were struck in the ninth and tenth centuries. The far greater number even of German, Bohemian, and other coins (Fig. 185), are proofs of commercial relations with southern lands. The majority belong to the latter half of the tenth century; all are of silver.

Not to speak of precious metals, introduced in the form of ingots, coins, and ornaments, we may consider as imports some damasked sword-blades and other remarkable weapons and fine stuffs. It is probable also that corn was imported when their own crops failed.

Fig. 185.—German silver coin. Gotl. ¼.[1]

The exports consisted chiefly of valuable skins, horses—the Swedish horses were specially famed—slaves, and possibly fish, wool, &c.

Commerce was carried on mainly by barter; the means of exchange or payment was gold or silver by weight. Weights and scales of this period have also been frequently found in Sweden. They were usually made of bronze, and are almost exactly like those now in use, with this difference, that the balance was so constructed that it could be folded up into three joints and put inside the two round cup-shaped scales (Fig. 186). It was thus possible to carry them about without any danger of breaking. The weights were often made of iron covered with a thin plating of bronze (Fig. 187). In this way any attempt to diminish the weight by filing was easily detected. The silver de-

---

[1] This coin was struck for the Emperor Otto III., whose name is inscribed between the arms of the cross. The back has his grandmother's and his guardian Athalhet's (or Adelheid's) names. The coin was struck somewhere about 991—995.

III.] THE IRON AGE. 193

signed as a means of payment was, like the gold so used in earlier times (see p. 129), often drawn out into thin

FIG. 186.—Pair of scales made of bronze. Upl. ⅛.

spirals.[1] The shape was convenient for handling, and they could be easily broken off into pieces of the size required. In the National Museum there are some spiral rings of this sort which may be regarded as in a certain sense "base coin," because they are made of copper covered with a very thin plating of silver. They remind us of

FIG. 187.—Iron weight plated with bronze. Gotl. ¼.

[1] The uncoined gold used for merchandise at the present day is often made in similar spirals.

O

the gold ring which King Olaf Tryggvason took from the temple-door at Lade, and which he afterwards gave as a great treasure to Queen Sigrid Storråda. "All praised the ring," Snorri Sturlason relates; "but two brothers, who were the queen's smiths, took it and weighed it in their hands, and then whispered to each other. When the queen asked them why they did so, they said that the ring was a cheat; whereupon she caused it to be broken asunder, and they found copper inside."[1]

For travelling in Sweden in ancient times they used as far as possible the many water-ways, because the roads, if indeed there were any, must have been still very bad. After the introduction of Christianity greater attention was paid to them, as we see among other things from the runic inscriptions, which speak of bridges or roads made for the souls of fathers, husbands, and sons by their surviving relatives.

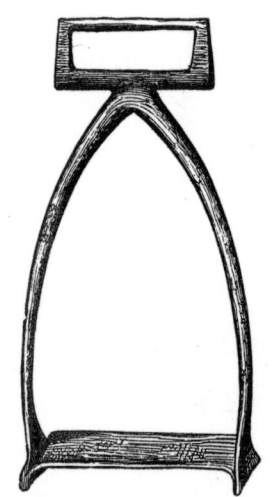

Fig. 188.—Iron stirrup. Upl. ⅓.

Upon a runic stone in Gotland is the figure of a plain cart with four wheels; and in some Swedish and Danish barrows of the end of the Iron Age not only were some bridles found together with spurs and stirrups (Fig. 188), but also bits of harness, in some cases remarkably beautiful. They were made of gilded bronze, and were tastefully decorated in a style peculiar to the North.

In fact a style had now been produced which was in

[1] See *Sea-Kings*, vol. i. p. 432.—Tr.]

III.] THE IRON AGE. 195

FIG. 189.—Bronze buckle. Skåne. ¼.

its origin due to an Irish influence, and which gradually developed into the beautiful "animal-interlacings" so well known to us from the runic stones (Figs. 204, 205) and the wooden churches of the earlier part of the Middle Ages. We have beautiful examples of this style of ornamentation in numbers of metal works belonging to the Viking Age found in Sweden, such as

Fig. 190.—Bronze plate. Gotl. ¾.

Fig. 191.—Gilded bronze plate that probably originally surrounded the foot of a drinking vessel. Gotl. ⅔.

gold and silver ornaments, silver vessels, bronze buckles (Fig. 189), shield-bosses, sword-hilts of gilded bronze, bronze chapes of sword-sheaths, &c., &c.

In Gotland especially examples of this style have been found in great abundance (see Figs. 190, 191). The finds in this island belonging to the last few centuries of heathendom are generally remarkable for the value of

III.] THE IRON AGE. 197

FIG. 192.—Bronze brooch. Gotl. ¼.

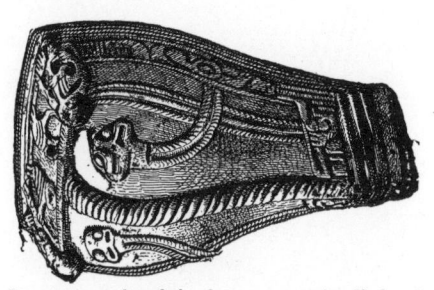

FIG. 193.—Bronze brooch, of the form of an animal's head. Gotl. ¼.

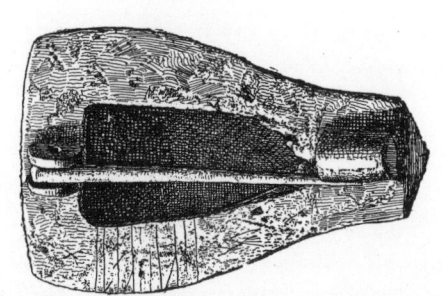

FIG. 194.—Back of Fig. 193, with a runic inscription.[1]

[1] The runes form the words INKI ISKATI in modern Swedish *Inge åt Åsgöt, i.e.* "Inge (made it) at Åsgöt."

their contents, and for the fact that many of the antiquities are of peculiar kinds not occurring in other parts of the North (Figs. 192—195). These grew out of the types usual during the earlier part of the Iron Age, the taste of an earlier time having here continued longer than on the mainland; just as at the present day the

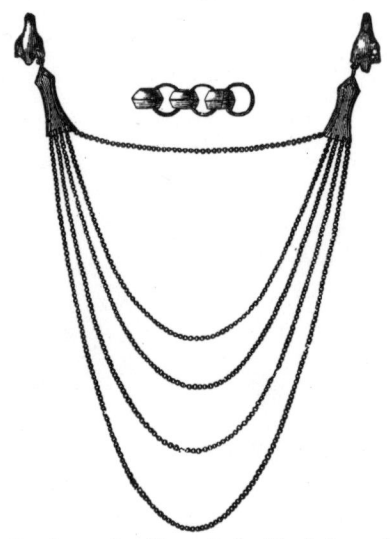

FIG. 195.—Two bronze buckles united with chains. Gotl. $\frac{1}{6}$ and $\frac{1}{4}$.

old Swedish language is far better preserved in Gotland than in most parts of Sweden.

The most popular temple of the ancient Swedes was that at Old Upsala, surrounded by its murky grove and its ancient barrows, of which the three great "kings'-barrows" already described are the largest.[1] In this temple the images of Thor, Woden, and Frey were placed.

[1] See above pp. 140, 141.

That the Northmen's artistic skill was during the heathen times actually employed in representing the Ása-gods in human forms is also proved by Snorri Sturlason's "Kings' Book." We there have described to us how Olaf Tryggvason, when he wanted to compel the Northmen to become Christians, went into a temple near Throndhjem. "When the king came to where the gods were, so it was that Thor sat there the most honoured of all the gods, adorned with gold

FIG. 196.—Gold bracteate. Gotl. ⅓.

and silver. The king lifted up a gold-headed stick which he had in his hand, and struck Thor, so that he fell down from off his pedestal. Thereupon the king's men leapt up and threw all the gods down from their pedestals."[1] And in St. Olaf's Saga we find the description of an image of Thor in a temple in the Norwegian Upland. "In his hand he holds a hammer. He is large of stature and hollow inside. Beneath him is a pedestal, where he stands when he is brought out.

[1 See *Sea-Kings*, vol. i. p. 440.—Tr.]

He has no lack of gold and silver upon him. Four cakes of bread are given him every day besides meat." When the image was broken in pieces, there came out "rats as large as cats, weasels, and serpents," which had thriven upon the food given to the god.[1]

There were not always temple-buildings at the place of sacrifice: often was it in the open air, in a sacred grove, or by a holy well, that the Swedes of heathen times celebrated their sacred rites.[2] Even if we pay no attention to tradition, we can at the present day reckon up a large number of places where the ancient Swedes sacrificed to the Ása-gods. Such are the frequently occurring place-names compounded with the words Hof, Harg, or Vi.[3] We can often further see to which god the place was consecrated. We have examples of this in Odensvi in Vestmanland and in Småland, Odensala in Upland, Thorsharg (now Thorshälla) in Södermanland, Thorslunda in Upland and in Öland (see pp. 121, 122), Frövi in Vestmanland, Frötuna in Upland, Ullevi in Upland and in Vestmanland, and others. The fact that so many of these now mark the place of Christian churches is worth noticing, because it shows that many parish churches in the country, just as the first cathedral at Upsala, were built upon the

[1] See *See-Kings*, vol. ii., pp. 158—160.—Tr.]
[2] There is reason to regard as places of sacrifice many of what are popularly known as "judgment-rings" or "judgment-seats," which are circles formed of large stones. The number of stones in such a circle is often nine. In the neighbourhood of these stones there are not unfrequently wells, some of which till quite recent times have been "offering-wells."
[3] The word *Hof* in heathen times corresponded very nearly with what we should now call "a temple," *Harg* to "an altar," and *Vi* to "a sanctuary" or "holy place."

same places which during heathendom were already devoted to sacred rites.

These place-names would be a further proof, if any

Fig. 197.—The "Ramsundsberg" with the "Sigurd-carving." Södermanl.

such were needed, that the ancient Swedes in the main worshipped the same gods and had the same religion as their relations in Norway and Iceland.

We also know that the heroic songs of the *Edda* were not unknown in Sweden. This we see from the remarkable figures which, together with runic inscriptions, are carved upon the "Ramsundsberg" in Jäder parish (Fig. 197), and the "Göksten" in Härad parish, both in West Södermanland. These represent several

FIG. 198.—Silver "Thor's hammer." Ö.-Götl. ¼.

scenes out of Sigurd Fafni's-bane's Saga. We here see the otter in the Andvara falls, and the smithy, tongs, hammer, and bellows belonging to the dwarf Regin. We see moreover how Sigurd slays the terrible dragon Fafni and roasts his heart over a fire. We have also here represented Sigurd's horse Grane laden with

Fafni's hoard, and the two hawks sitting in a tree, from whose conversation Sigurd learns the treachery with which he is threatened by the cunning and revengeful Regin. Regin himself also, who was murdered on this account by Sigurd, is seen with his head off.[1]

We have also traces of the heathen worship of the ancient Swedes in the not uncommon, sometimes richly decorated, silver pendents which occur in finds of the later Iron Age. These were doubtless intended to represent Thor's hammer, and were worn in token of the worship of Thor in the same way as the crucifix is worn by Christians (Fig. 198).

Of the details of their religious belief, of education, marriage, and other institutions connected with the home-life in Sweden during heathen times we have no particular knowledge, except so far as it can be gathered by a comparison with what we know of the contemporary condition of Norway and Iceland, and from the customs described in the most ancient laws of Sweden. But as the latter in their present state point directly only to the thirteenth and fourteenth centuries, and as the contents of the Eddas and Icelandic Sagas are fairly accessible, we have not thought it worth while to dwell further on this branch of our subject, enticing though it be. Besides, the description it would involve would carry us far beyond the limits proposed for our present work.

We can however through numerous finds get *direct* evidence concerning the customs of burial in Sweden during the Viking Period. These finds prove that the

[1 For this legend see *Corp. Bor.*, vol. i., pp. 31 and following, and for a modern reproduction of it *The Story of Sigurd the Volsung*, by William Morris.—Tr.]

204 ANCIENT SWEDISH CIVILISATION. [CHAP.

FIG. 199.—Barrow from the Viking Period. Södermanl.

dead were sometimes burnt and were sometimes inhumed. Both these customs existed side by side in Sweden during the Later Iron Age, though in certain tracts, as especially round the Mälar lake, cremation seems to have been the most usual practice.

If the corpse was to be burnt, it was usually laid fully-clad upon the pyre with weapons and ornaments; hence we usually find these much injured from the effects of the fire (see p. 122). Not unfrequently horses, dogs, falcons, or other pet animals, possibly even thralls also, were slain and laid by the side of their master upon the pyre. The ashes and fragments of bone were afterwards often deposited in an earthen vessel. The graves were either covered by a barrow, or marked with stones ranged in a circle or a triangle or in the form of a ship pointed at both ends (Figs. 199—201).

The Sagas give us many accounts of men who were "set in barrows in their ships." We have already spoken of graves which bear out this description at Ulltuna, Vendel, Tune, and Gokstad.

Out of an old Saga we get the following description of King Harald Hildetand's burial:—"The day after the battle of Brávalla, King Sigurd Ring bade them find Harald's body, wipe off the blood, and lay it out honourably after ancient custom. He bade them place it on the chariot which Harald had used in the battle. Then he bade them cast up a great barrow, and made Harald drive into the barrow with the same horse which he had used in the fight. After that was the horse slain, and King Sigurd bade them take the saddle in which he had ridden himself, and he gave it to King Harald, and bade him do whichever he pleased, either ride to Valhalla or drive thither. Before the

Fig. 200.—Grave-stones arranged in the form of a ship; near Blomsholm in Bohuslän.

barrow was closed up, King Sigurd bade all mighty men and warriors to cast in thither great rings and good weapons to the honour of King Harald Hildetand."

Although this account cannot be trusted in every detail, yet it is of great importance, because in the graves inside the barrows there have often been found traces of horses, bridles, stirrups, and harness.

Unburnt bodies of this period are often found lying in stone or wooden coffins; sometimes they are found however without any now visible traces of any such protection. In several barrows belonging to this time, especially in Norway, there are chambers built of wood, in which the corpses were sometimes laid upon stuffed cushions or sometimes seated on chairs (see p. 151 and note). The most remarkable grave of this kind yet known in the North is that of Queen Thyra in one of the great barrows at Jellinge in Jutland, dating from about 950. The grave-chamber is 21 ft. 6in. long, 8 ft. broad, and 4 ft. 5in. high, and is made of oak trunks and boarded inside with planks of the same wood. The walls had been hung with woollen stuffs.

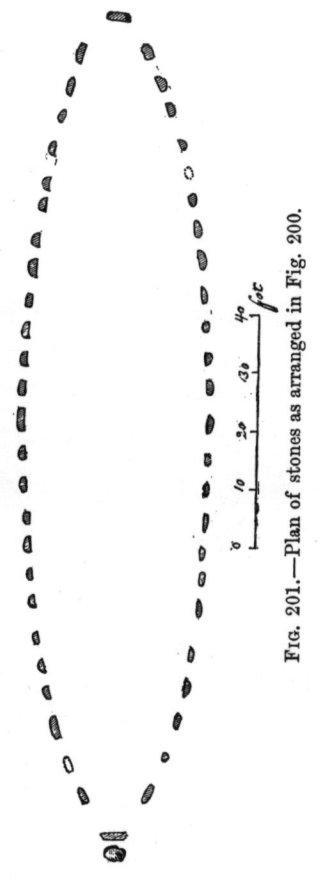

FIG. 201.—Plan of stones as arranged in Fig. 200.

To the memory of the dead they often raised what are called "bauta-stones" (see Fig. 202); but only where they have written upon them the name of their departed friend has it been preserved to us. The names were of course always written in runes. This method of writing was certainly, as we have seen, known in the North shortly after the beginning of the Christian era; but most of the runic inscriptions—of which

Fig. 202.—Barrow with "bauta-stone" near Gödestad in Halland.

in Upland alone there are more than a thousand—belong to the end of the Viking Period (Figs. 203—205). It seems therefore as though it was only just at the end of the Viking Period that the custom came into general use of thus giving to themselves and their friends a more permanent memorial than tradition alone could give.

The writing of the Later Iron Age, or the "later runes" as they are called, are very different from those used during the preceding period. The later set of runes, which however nearly agrees with the earlier in the order of the letters, comprises only the following sixteen :—

ᚠ ᚢ ᚦ ᚩ ᚱ ᚴ : ᚼ ᚾ ᛁ ᛆ ᛌ : ᛐ ᛒ ᛚ ᛘ ᛦ
f u th o r k : h n i a s : t b l m -r

The rune ᛦ is generally used, like ᛦ of the earlier runes, at the end of a word, and then corresponds to our *r*; but sometimes it occurs also in the middle of a word, in which case it represents a vowel sound—usually *y*, but occasionally *e* or *œ*. The runes ᚩ, ᚼ, ᛁ, ᚾ, ᛐ, and ᛦ, have also the following forms : ᛆ or ᚴ = *o*, ᚾ = *n*, ᛆ = *a*, ᛁ = *s*, ᛐ = *t*, and ᛙ = *m*. After the end of what were properly heathen times, especially, they often used the symbols known as "pointed runes," ᚽ = *y*, ᚵ = *g*, ᛂ = *e*, ᛄ = *d*, and ᛔ = *p*. In order to spare space they sometimes made one "stem"—as the upright stroke was called—do for two runes; thus, for example, ᛰ, ᛲ, and others were combined to make what are called "double runes."

The word "rune" seems properly to mean "secrecy," and it was long considered a wonderful secret how one man could by such simple strokes communicate his thoughts to another. From this it was a natural step to attribute to runes a secret magic power; and so we have pretty frequent accounts of their use as charms. Thus we read in the *Edda*,[1] how Brynhild by the following words taught Sigurd "Fafni's-bane" the virtue of the runes—

"Victory-runes" must thou know,
if thou wilt victory gain.

[1 *Corp. Poet. Bor.*, i., pp. 40, 41.—Tr.]

> Cut them on thy sword-hilt.[1]
> Others cut upon the blade
> and twice name Tyr.[2]
> Storm-runes must thou cut,
> if thou wilt guarded have
> thy ship in the breaker's roar.
> Cut them upon the stem
> and eke the rudder's blade.
> Thought-runes must thou know,
> Wilt thou than others wiser be.
> Woden hath these runes,
> Himself devised . . . .

The use of runes by slow degrees gave way to the letters of the Latin alphabet introduced with Christianity. Yet many still preserved Christian grave-stones, fonts, church-bells, thuribles, and other things with runic inscriptions show that their use long survived the final establishment of the new religion. In certain out-of-the-way districts they were still in memory after the Reformation, and on the "runic staves," or ancient "club-almanacs" runes were still cut only a hundred years ago. During the Middle Ages whole books were actually written with runes, as, for example, the still preserved Laws of Skåne, dating from the thirteenth century.

The runic stone richly adorned with beautiful "animal-interlacings" which is represented in Fig. 204 stands on Viggby farm in the parish of Lillkyrka in Upland. The inscription, which begins in the middle of the bottom row, reads in ordinary letters thus: *Bruni lit risa auk*

---

[1] At Gilton, in the English county of Kent, they found a sword with runes engraved on the hilt (*cf.* also p. 119). [Gilton is in the parish of Ash near Sandwich—Tr.]

[2] Tyr was the name of one of the Åsa-gods, and also of the rune ↑.

aristin[1] *thina yftir Kuth fast fathur Bruna auk Arnuitir*[2] *buanta sin.* In modern Swedish it would

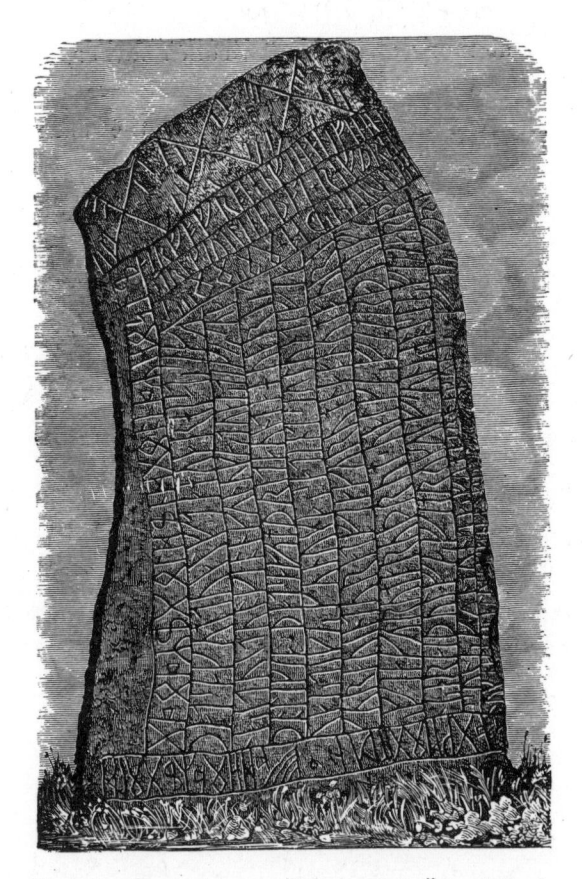

FIG. 203.—Runic-stone near Rök church in Öster-Götland.

[1] Instead of *arist(a) stin.* They avoided the repetition of the same letters as much as possible. To such an extent was this carried out that, if a word began with the same rune or runes with which the preceding word ended, the two words were joined together, and the common runes only inscribed once. Sometimes a rune was entirely left out, if the connexion of sense was not thereby lost. [2] Instead of *Arnui i(f)tir.*

be : *Brune lät resa och rista sten denna efter Gudfast, fader Brunes, och Arnvi efter bonde (i.e., make) sin,* and means " Brune caused this stone to be raised and engraved in memory of Gudfast, Brune's father, and Arnvi in memory of her husband."

In many cases we not only know the name of the

FIG. 204.—Runic-stone at Viggby in Upland, 7 ft. high.

man who had the memorial raised, and of the person in whose honour it was raised, but also that of the man who engraved the runes and carved the often very skilful and artistic interlacings. The best known of these " rune masters," if we may call them so, are *Ypper*

III.] THE IRON AGE. 213

(the old form is Ubir), whose name appears upon Fig. 205 and some forty other runic stones, Bale, Åsmund Kåresson, Thorbjörn Skald, &c., who all worked in Upland and the neighbouring districts.

Most of the rune-carvers seem to have lived at a time when the Åsa-gods and the "White Christ" were contending with each other for the mastery in Sweden.

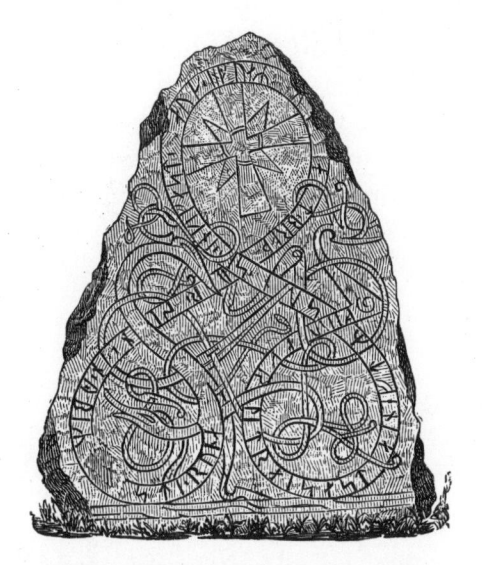

FIG. 205.—Runic-stone near Vik in Upland.[1]

We cannot here describe the progress of this wonderful contest, which only after many vicissitudes ended in the victory of the new learning. So deep however was the

[1] The inscription on Fig. 205 runs as follows: *Kiulakr lit raisa stain eftir sun sin Inkifast auk Inkuar [h]uk at brothur sin. In Ubir [ri]sti runa.* In modern Swedish: *Gjulak lät resa sten efter son sin Ingefast, och Ingvar högg åt broder sin. Men Ypper ristade runorna.* —" Gjulak caused [this] stone to be raised to the memory of his son Ingefast, and Ingvar set it up to his brother. But Ypper carved the runes."

old faith rooted in the mind of the people, that even in the present day, a thousand years after Christianity was first preached in the country, many traces of the old heathen superstitions survive. These perhaps may shortly die out; for they can hardly withstand the light spread by a sound and universal education of the people. But what we hope may never die out so long as a free people is born and bred in our land, is the love of freedom, the power, and the heroism which distinguished the Northmen during heathen times, and the pure purpose of life, which secured their religion a high place among the pre-Christian religions, the wisdom which does not make the chief business of life the enjoyment of earthly pleasures, but seeks it in Valhalla, in the Allfather's Hall.

THE END.